Wates's Book of
LONDON
CHURCHYARDS

HARVEY HACKMAN

WATES'S BOOK OF
LONDON CHURCHYARDS

WATES'S BOOK OF
LONDON
CHURCHYARDS

*A Guide to
the Old Churchyards and Burial-grounds of
the City and Central London*

HARVEY HACKMAN

COLLINS
St James's Place, London
1981

William Collins Sons & Co Ltd
London · Glasgow · Sydney · Auckland
Toronto · Johannesburg

First published 1981
© Harvey Hackman 1981
ISBN 0 00 216313 6
Filmset in Monophoto Bembo
Made and Printed in Great Britain by
William Collins Sons & Co Ltd, Glasgow

CONTENTS

LIST OF ILLUSTRATIONS

*All illustrations except those separately credited above are by Angelo
Hornak*

As builders and developers our daily work is changing the face and shape of London. On occasions we preserve the best of the old, on others we have such confidence in the superiority of our designs and building techniques over those of preceding ages that we destroy the past and replace it with our own buildings.

These buildings will, we believe, be seen in later years as eloquent statements about the values and standards held by the men who built them.

Judgement of our work will hardly take account of the political and commercial constraints under which we operate, nor will it recognize the fickle shifts of conservation fashion.

Amongst the most arbitrary but most fortunate of the beneficiaries of these constraints are the Churchyards of London, which Mr Hackman describes with such scholarship in this guide.

CHRISTOPHER WATES
Chief Executive
Wates Limited

FOREWORD

by Simon Jenkins

The old churchyard is now a tiny well of sunlight sunk deep beneath a plateau of City office blocks. Its grass is green-black and tough as wire, with roots buried in a rancid compost of leaves, soot and London clay. Across it, the soles of City feet drum a relentless march, as if to stamp it into oblivion. Round stand the sentinels of the place, headstones of long-departed citizens laughingly bidding their successors to rest in peace. These stones are now distributed more for their own protection than for the dignity of their original purpose. The acid London air has eaten into their inscriptions and carried all memory of their subjects to the winds. Overhead squadrons of starlings and sparrows dispute the time of day with a scavenging pigeon. A lanky plane tree is their gymnasium, its bark scarred from a hundred seasons battling against the City atmosphere. Its broad leaves permit only the meagrest drops of rain and sun to make the long journey down to the grass below. To one side is an old bench, dusted each lunchtime by anonymous metropolitan backsides to the benefit of the two old tramps for whom it is the one true home. They know every grain and splinter. Against the church wall is a shed containing a broom, spade and weeding fork, emblems of office for the modern sexton, the Corporation gardener. The City fathers have allowed him a splash of geraniums, adding a gaudy touch of rouge to the wizened face of the old flowerbed.

London's churchyards are enchanting. No modern city has their equal. They are monuments to the city's longevity and continuity and are today the strongest link with its medieval past. Almost all the gardens mentioned in this book are of pre-Reformation origin. They have survived in a limbo of church law, protected by exclusion from countless Acts of Parliament, consecrated, desecrated, hallowed and unhallowed, but never quite disowned. Since before the Great Fire, they have lived in a nether world of parish clerks, vestries, liveried companies, aldermen and ecclesiastical lawyers, so numerous and fusty that any case touching on their boundaries makes Jarndyce and Jarndyce seem like summary justice. A church itself is a building which can in due course be deconsecrated, demolished and redeveloped. But God's acre is inhabited still by the souls of departed citizens. Lay a finger on that and all the hobgoblins of Temple Lane will storm down Fleet Street and consume you in a hell-fire of legal fees. With primogeniture and Crown privilege, church law stands on the escutcheon of the British constitution as testament to our freedom from revolutionary upheaval.

The churchyards are medieval not only in origin but also in shape. I know of none which is either a true square or a circle. Shapeless polygons, their borders owe nothing to the planner's set-square or the laws of geometry. They seem to have been pushed, squeezed, sliced or moulded between office block, church wall and pavement, and sometimes even lifted bodily into the air and dumped somewhere completely different, like some unwanted old baggage who refuses to die. To modern architects or quantity surveyors, they are a natural hazard, a disaster. They must be faced as a navigator faces a magnetic storm, an act of God which for a while must defy all science. They are true relics of medieval archaeology.

Other English cities which possessed a large number of pre-Reformation churches, such as York, Lincoln and Norwich, have seen most of them vanish. London once had some 140 medieval places of worship yet of these over half remain today in some shape or form. Though many of their churchyards have disappeared, the yards of other vanished churches (such as St Martin Outwich and St Anne, Blackfriars) have actually survived in compensation. In his fascinating treasure hunt, Harvey Hackman has unearthed no fewer than seventy of these yards, including some churchyards and burial-grounds in the old City of Westminster and neighbouring villages.

The story of these places is the story of London. Though each may once have held the aura of timeless sanctuary still possessed by country churchyards, they soon became crowded repositories for the urban dead, bursting from the confines of old church vaults. The sixteenth- and seventeenth-century plagues saw corpses not so much buried as tossed into graveyards. During the Great Plague of 1665, the authorities merely heaped lime on the piles of bodies, raising the levels of many London churchyards by two or three feet (St Helen, Bishopsgate, for instance, or that most Dickensian of yards at St Bartholomew the Great). By the early nineteenth century, all peace and gentility had fled the churchyards and their vicinity for the cleaner air of the suburbs. Graves were dug over and over, bodies were crammed on top of each other, stolen for dissection or merely shifted back and forth. Many Londoners moved more often after their death than when still living.

City graveyards became an earthly manifestation of hell, a breeding ground of disease avoided by all but those whose poverty left them no option. To Dickens they supplied some of his most graphic images of urban squalor: 'so pressed upon by houses; so small, so rank, so forgotten except by the few people who ever look down on them from their smokey windows. As I stand peeping in through the iron gates and rails, I can peel the rusty metal off, like bark from an old tree ... one of my best-loved I call the churchyard of St Ghastly Grim' (*Sketches by Boz*). The tale of the churchyards' rescue from this horror is told in Hackman's own introduction: the Chadwick reforms and the Burial Acts which led in the 1850s to the banning of all inner London burials and the development of suburban cemeteries and crematoria. Here in the private mausolea of Kensal Green and Highgate, Brompton and Nunhead, arose the great monuments of the Victorian way of death. Their fantastic catacombs and pious mottoes, garishly decorated with coloured marble, with motifs classical, Gothic and baroque and with arts nouveau and deco, are as distant from our City churchyards as a modern new town is from a smugglers' cove.

Some of these new cemeteries were out-of-town parish burial-grounds, still linked to a church in London or Westminster. Others were run by private companies for often considerable private profit. In departing the city, they undoubtedly took with them much of the ceremony and sense of purpose of the former churchyards, leaving the latter dejected and often squalid refuse tips. (Indeed of the yards covered in this book, only the Nonconformist burial-ground of Bunhill Fields, with its magnificent chest tombs, still has a true graveyard atmosphere – and that, ironically, was never attached to any church.) Yet still they survived. Some admittedly

13

have become little more than verges between church walls and roaring traffic. But most have been taken into municipal care, undergoing a slow transmogrification from religious sanctuary to symbol of civic pride. They have been tidied and replanted, their headstones moved to the perimeter, seats placed along paths coated with alien asphalt (rather than honest York stone) and robust exotics from Kew arranged in tasteful boxes.

Yet they have never totally surrendered to this antiseptic. Those who look on London's churchyards as 'amenities' will miss the point – they should go instead to the sweeping spaces of the royal parks or the genteel groves of West London's avenues and private squares. City churchyards are for connoisseurs of urban struggle, of the battle between past and present and between nature and the more offensive works of man. They have been fighting, some of them, for seven or eight centuries. Their rolls of honour are carved on the plaques, memorials and gravestones which still breath history into their neat paths –

> 'The parish names cut deep and strong
> To hold the shades of evening long' (Betjeman).

Each mounts its individual defences. The yard of St Clement Danes rises like a bow wave round Wren's sturdy galleon as it braves the winds of verbiage pouring at it down Fleet Street, the good Dr Johnson standing valiant as its figurehead. The yard of St Mary-at-Hill is like a castle dungeon, so grim that even the ghosts must shudder and flee at nightfall. At St Andrew, Holborn, a burst of civic horticulture is rising towards the battlements as if the flora itself were intent on becoming an outer bailey. Giant planes alone guard the crippled corpse of St Anne, Soho, while the yard of the actors' church, St Paul, Covent Garden, has withdrawn altogether, tortoise-like behind its walls and iron railings.

No one would have proposed or planned these places. No modern town or city would think of creating them. They are unintended, unobtrusive oases of natural sound, of leaves rustling, birds chattering, humans murmuring to each other above the cacophony of mechanical combustion. They are havens in which executives and their clerks alike ride out the storms of City business. Here secretaries find relief from tedium, workmen relax on cool grass and children escape from nagging discipline. They are good places, and magical ones.

My own first London office looked down on the churchyard of St Anne, Blackfriars. The abbey, which once stood by the mouth of the old Fleet ditch, had long ago vanished but its yard, once the nave of the abbey itself, remained as a forgotten pool hidden among the buildings south of Carter Lane. Into that pool I used to throw my dreams, as thousands of City workers must have done before. I would stir them in among its stones, nourishing them in summer with the few rays of sunlight which managed to reach its depths. At night, when I was last in the office and the lights were out, those dreams would come to life and dance with the spirits of Londoners long dead, as they whirled back and forth down the seven ages of the City. It wanted only the magic lamplighter and his wand. For it is in such places that our past becomes our present.

INTRODUCTION

Several London churchyards have Roman remains. In the green on the north side of Westminster Abbey, which is now merged with the churchyard of St Margaret's, was found a Roman sarcophagus. Parts of the Roman wall are incorporated in the churchyards of St Alphage, London Wall and All Hallows, London Wall. The church of Old St Pancras was built on the site of a Roman shrine. St Peter, Cornhill claims to have been founded in AD 179 and there are a number of churches of Saxon origin. The last churches to be built with their own churchyards were St Luke, Sydney Street, Chelsea (consecrated 1824) and Holy Trinity, Brompton (consecrated 1829). Burials had ceased by 1855. The span is over a thousand years.

Traces of the history of London appear everywhere in the story of its churchyards and burial-grounds. Invasion, Rebellion, Treason, Plague, Fire, Famine and Religious Disputes all have their place. This is particularly true of the churches within the City walls. It is round St Paul's that the tide of history flowed most strongly but there are many others which added their contributions – St Magnus the Martyr standing where old London Bridge left the City, St Bartholomew the Great before which the martyrs were burnt, St Sepulchre-without-Newgate just across the street from the notorious gaol, All Hallows, Barking which offered a temporary resting place to the bodies of some who had died on Tower Hill, St Giles-in-the-Fields where felons on their last journey to Tyburn were sustained with a draught of ale, and St Olave, Hart Street where Samuel Pepys and the Navy Board worshipped. Then there is the great Nonconformist burial-ground at Bunhill Fields, with its small neighbour the Quaker burial-ground. These have not such a long history, being established in the seventeenth century for the growing number of those whom nonconformity excluded from burial within a parish churchyard, but many distinguished names are recorded here.

Outside the City walls in Westminster and the neighbouring villages there were churches just as old as those in the City. St Pancras was recognized as a parish as early as the ninth century and the church of St Clement Danes in the Strand has a history almost as long. The first churches of St Margaret, Westminster, Chelsea Old Church, St Mary Abbots, Kensington, St Giles-in-the-Fields, St Marylebone, St Martin-in-the-Fields and St Mary, Paddington Green were all founded before the end of the thirteenth century. Remains of the churchyards of all these churches still survive.

As the years passed by the number of churches within the City decreased. A church would become derelict or be burnt down (the early churches were usually built of wood), two parishes would be united and the old church not rebuilt. The most serious loss occurred in the Great Fire of 1666 when eighty-eight out of the City's 108 churches were destroyed. Thirty-five were not rebuilt. Nevertheless in several cases their churchyards continued in use until the nineteenth century. On the other hand the number of churchyards outside the City continued to grow. As the City spread westwards towards Westminster new churches such as St Paul, Covent Garden, St James, Piccadilly and St Anne, Soho, were built to meet the needs of the new residential areas. Older churches acquired new burial-grounds away from their churchyards. In 1668 St Martin-in-the-Fields bought a large ground on the south side of Irving Street (then known as Dirty Lane) for this purpose. St James, Piccadilly bought land in the Hampstead Road. This practice was extended when the new churches promoted by Queen Anne were being built at the beginning of the eighteenth century. St George, Bloomsbury, St George the Martyr, Queen's Square, St George, Hanover Square and St John, Smith Square all acquired land away from their churches. It was at about this time too that it became necessary to provide places of burial with watch-towers and watchmen to protect them from the activities of the body-snatchers seeking corpses to sell for medical research.

It was not until late in the eighteenth century that coffins came into general use. Moreover most distinguished parishioners were buried within the church, although, as the grave-maker at St Bride's told Samuel Pepys, it was sometimes necessary to 'jostle them together to make room'. It would seem that, except in times of disaster such as the Black Death of 1348 and the various other visitations of the plague, when special provision had to be made for burying the dead, churchyards with their additional burial-grounds were able to accommodate their parishioners.

The population explosion which took place between 1801 and 1851 altered all this. During this period the population of England increased from 8,893,000 to 17,928,000 – over one hundred per cent. It should not have been necessary to await these figures before taking action, but as usual the British were slow to recognize danger. It was only in 1832 that the first Act of Parliament authorizing the creation of a cemetery – at Kensal Green – was passed, nor did this prevent the continuation of burial within urban churchyards, particularly amongst the poor. It is curious that both French and American thought was well ahead of the British. As early as 1777 a plan was formulated in Paris to abolish all the existing places of burial and to transfer their contents to the catacombs. Effect was given to this plan in 1786, and in 1790 the use of existing burial-grounds was forbidden throughout France. The famous Père Lachaise cemetery was opened in 1804. At about the same time the Board of Health in New York appointed a committee to advise what steps should be taken with a view to prohibiting burial within the boundaries of the City.

In England many horrors were to be perpetrated and many unnecessary deaths caused before any such action was taken. It was not until 1842 that, propelled by public agitation led by Dr G. A. Walker, a surgeon practising in Drury Lane, the House of Commons set up a Select Committee to study the position. The evidence which the Committee heard was described as horrible and sickening and it is hard to credit today. Not only were corpses pressed into graveyards which could not accommodate them, but bodies were removed soon after burial to make way for others. As Dr Walker wrote of St Giles's churchyard, 'Here in this place of "Christian burial", you may see human heads, covered with hair; and, here, in this "consecrated ground", are human bones with flesh still adhering to them.' The evidence with regard to burial within vaults was even more horrific. Bodies were packed below, sometimes separated from the place of worship above by only a boarded floor. Witnesses testified that the rate of mortality amongst families living near such places was three times as high as in other parts of the parish. Charles Dickens, when describing the burial of Mr Krook's lodger in *Bleak House*, wrote of the burial-ground of St Mary-le-Strand as 'a hemmed-in churchyard, pestiferous and obscene, whence malignant diseases are communicated to the bodies of our dear brothers and sisters who have not departed.'

In due course, some ten years later, the findings of the Select Committee led to the passing of the first of the Burial Acts in 1852, under which burials in the Metropolis were to be discontinued by Order in Council. This was followed by further Acts in 1853, 1854 and 1855. By this date burial within a town or city had virtually ceased. Vestries were required to provide new burial-grounds and were made responsible for the maintenance in decent order of any churchyard or burial-ground which had been closed. The effect of the Burial Acts was however largely negative. Whilst they prevented the churchyards from being used for burial, they did not prescribe how they should be used. Indeed it was difficult to see to what immediate use, beneficial to members of the public, they could be put. For a number of years they remained, for the most part, little more than dumping grounds for rubbish and a hunting ground for stray cats and vermin.

From the time of its closure it had always been possible for the incumbent to try to make better use of his churchyard, as did the Rev William Rogers at St Botolph, Bishopsgate, but initially there was little enthusiasm. By 1877 seven disused burial-grounds had been converted into public gardens. By 1884 of 404 known burial-grounds in London forty-one were in use as gardens, twenty-seven were in private ownership, twenty-one were still in use as places of burial under exceptions to the General Orders for Closure, ninety-seven had been sold for building sites or in some way absorbed into surrounding properties, eight more were under offer for sale as building sites, and 210 remained closed and unused or derelict. The eight which were on offer for sale were saved by the passing of the Disused Burial Grounds Act in 1884, which forbade building (except for church purposes) on burial-grounds which had been closed. This Act was to a great extent the work of Lord Brabazon (subsequently the Earl of Meath) who had formed, in 1882, what is today the 'Metropolitan Public Gardens Association'. The main objective of this body was the conversion of 'all disused burial-grounds, waste places and enclosed squares' into 'resting places, gardens and playgrounds'.

The formation of the Association and the passing of the 1884 Act heralded a new era in the story of the London churchyards. In its first report presented in October 1883 the Association recorded nine burial-grounds converted into gardens including those of St John's Wood Chapel (as it then was) and Old St Pancras, together with thirty-three more in hand or planned, including the churchyards of the Chapel Royal, Savoy, St Margaret, Westminster, St Paul's Cathedral, St Giles-in-the-Fields, St John the Evangelist, Drury Lane and the burial-grounds of Holy Trinity, Gray's Inn Road, St George the Martyr, Bloomsbury, St George, Hanover Square and Bunhill Fields. By 1892 the number of conversions had risen to 104, and by 1912 to 135.

All churchyard gardens are now maintained by the local authority unless the garden still remains in the hands of the incumbent, when the work is done by the verger or by parish volunteers. The activities of the Association however continue. After the 1939–45 War it was responsible for the introduction of Rest Gardens in a number of churchyards by way of War Memorials, and also for the restoration of churchyards damaged by the air raids. Today it acts as judge in the Church Gardens Competition, which was instituted in 1957 by the Worshipful Company of Gardeners at the instigation of the then Bishop of Woolwich the Right Reverend R. W. Stannard.

With the development of the gardens during the twentieth century the tombstones have tended to disappear. With one or two notable exceptions, of which Bunhill Fields is the most striking, they have either been removed altogether or have been relegated to paving the footpath or supporting the surrounding walls. In some cases one or two stones have been left, no doubt as a discernible reminder of the original purpose of the place in which they stand. Even where the stones remain the London weather hastens the decay of the inscriptions. As it is more than one hundred and twenty years since the last inscriptions were cut it is not surprising that few are now legible; where they are, it usually means that they have been re-cut. Fortunately in many instances records of the inscriptions were made whilst they could still be read. Some of these were made by local authorities, others by enthusiastic amateurs, such as Dr John Rippon who transcribed all the inscriptions on the tombstones in Bunhill Fields before he died in 1836, or

Mr Percy Rushden who published in 1910 *The Churchyard Inscriptions of the City of London*, wherein he recorded several hundred inscriptions from fifty-nine former places of burial within the City. Such a feat would no longer be possible.

Today there are seventy-three churchyard gardens in the City and Central London which can be visited. Some like St Paul, Bunhill Fields, St Botolph, Aldersgate (generally known as 'Postman's Park') and St Mary, Paddington Green are large areas with much to see; others are minute and have little to tell. Some like St Bartholomew's the Great, St Margaret, Westminster, and the Queen's Chapel of the Savoy are redolent of history, whilst others like St Mary-le-Bow and St Michael, Cornhill have their own local anecdotes to tell. For many the churchyard gardens will remain simply a pleasant place in which to eat a lunchtime sandwich or to sit and rest a while, but each garden can also offer some particle of the nation's history to those who wish to find it.

ALL HALLOWS, BARKING
(generally known as All Hallows-by-the-Tower),
TOWER HILL EC3

There is still a good garden left here, but, as is usually the case, it is much smaller than the original churchyard, which was extensive and surrounded the church on its north, south and east sides.

When the Abbey of Barking was founded by Erkenwald, Bishop of London (671–8), for his sister Ethelburga, he made to it a grant of land in the City of London, on which the first church of All Hallows, Barking was built. On the northern part of this land Richard Coeur de Lion sub-sequently built a chapel to St Mary – in which medieval tradition said that his heart was buried. Certainly this chapel enjoyed royal patronage, and the brotherhood which was attached to it was of considerable import-ance until the chapel was pulled down in 1548 after the Reformation. Stow* says that during the remainder of the century the land, which was cleared, was used as a garden plot until 'a store house of merchants goods brought from the sea by Sir William Winter etc.' was built on it. This appears to have been the first encroachment but it is plain that over the centuries a great deal more of the churchyard disappeared in similar ways. Another part on the south side was lost when Tower Street was widened in the nineteenth century.

Today's garden lies to the east of the church – a small portion retaining the aspect of a churchyard. This contains the family vault of Joseph Steele of Cumberland 'upward of 70 years an inhabitant of this parish, died September 1835, in his 90th year', of his brother Henry Steele, whose body

* *Survey of London*, 1603 Edition. Reprinted Everyman Library 1965.

was transferred from St Andrew Undershaft; and also the tomb of Samuel Gittens M.D., 'son of Samuel and Mary Gittens of Barbadoes died 5 July 1777 in his 20th year'. The larger part of the churchyard has been laid out as a terrace garden and is known as 'Tower Hill Terrace'. It was constructed by the Tower Hill Improvement Trust in 1951. It commands a good view of the Tower and Tower Hill.

As the churchyard was so close to the place of execution on Tower Hill it was used for temporary burials. On 22 July 1535 Bishop John Fisher was buried 'in the churchyard of Barkyn by the northe door'; but when Sir Thomas More was executed shortly afterwards the Bishop was taken up again and they were both buried in the Tower. In 1547 Henry Howard, Earl of Surrey, the poet, was buried here; in 1614 his body was removed to Framlingham. Lord Thomas Grey, the uncle of Lady Jane Grey, was buried here in April 1554. The body of Archbishop Laud remained here from the time of his execution in January 1645 until he too was moved – in 1663 to St John's College, Oxford. Amongst those who did not come via Tower Hill were William Thinne (died 1546), one of the Clerks of the Green Cloth and Master of the Household of Henry VIII, who published the first edition of the works of Chaucer, and William Armorer (died 1560), clothworker (and maker of the King's shirts), Governor of the pages of honour or master of the heance men, who served four Sovereigns – Henry VIII, Edward VI, Queen Mary, and Queen Elizabeth – over a period of fifty-one years.

ALL HALLOWS, LONDON WALL EC2

The most interesting feature of this small garden, which lies to the west of the church tower along the north side of London Wall, is its association with the old wall. A section of the Roman wall underlies the north wall of the church and the vestry is circular because it conforms to the shape of the Roman bastion beneath it. The medieval wall runs west from the church forming the northern boundary of the churchyard garden. When excavations were made in the churchyard in 1905 brick-lined Roman culverts were found in the base of the wall which Nikolaus Pevsner considers to have been for the passage of branches of the Walbrook.

St Anne, Soho. Churchyard and the tower which survived the Blitz.

Tomb of the Revd. Basil
Woodd by J. C. F. Rossi.
St Mary, Paddington
Green.

Tombstone of William
Hazlitt – Painter and
Essayist. St Anne, Soho.

METROPOLITAN POLICE ... CRICKETTS ...
DROWNED AT TEIGNMOUTH
WHILST TRYING TO RESCUE
A BOY BATHING AND SEEN
TO BE IN DIFFICULTY
· 11 · SEPT · 1916 ·

P.C. EDWARD GEORGE
BROWN GREENOFF
METROPOLITAN POLICE
MANY LIVES WERE SAVED BY HIS
DEVOTION TO DUTY AT THE
TERRIBLE EXPLOSION AT
SILVERTOWN · 19 · JAN · 1917

P·C·PERCY EDWIN COOK
METROPOLITAN POLICE
VOLUNTARILY DESCENDED HIGH
TENSION CHAMBER AT KENSINGTON
TO RESCUE TWO WORKMEN
OVERCOME BY POISONOUS GAS
· 7 · OCT · 1927 ·

FREDERICK MILLS·A·RUTTER
ROBERT DURRANT & F·D·JONES
WHO LOST THEIR LIVES IN
BRAVELY STRIVING TO SAVE
A COMRADE AT THE SEWAGE
PUMPING WORKS · EAST HAM ·
JULY · 1ST · 1895

ELIZABETH BOXALL
AGED 17 OF BETHNAL GREEN
WHO DIED OF INJURIES RECEIVED
IN TRYING TO SAVE
A CHILD
FROM A RUNAWAY HORSE
JUNE · 20 · 1888

HERBERT PETER CAZALY
STATIONER'S CLERK
WHO WAS DROWNED AT KEW
IN ENDEAVOURING TO SAVE
A MAN FROM DROWNING
APRIL 21 1889

HERBERT MACONOGHU
SCHOOL BOY FROM WIMBLEDON AGED 13
· HIS PARENTS ABSENT IN INDIA · LOST ·
HIS LIFE IN VAINLY TRYING TO RESCUE
· HIS TWO SCHOOL FELLOWS WHO WERE ·
· DROWNED AT GLOVERS POOL · CROYDE ·
NORTH DEVON · AUGUST · 28 · 1882

SAMUEL RABBETH
MEDICAL OFFICER
OF THE ROYAL FREE HOSPITAL
WHO TRIED TO SAVE A CHILD
SUFFERING FROM DIPHTHERIA
AT THE COST OF HIS OWN LIFE
OCTOBER 26 1884

FREDERICK ALFRED CROFT
INSPECTOR · AGED 31
SAVED A LUNATIC WOMAN
FROM SUICIDE AT WOOLWICH
ARSENAL STATION · BUT WAS
HIMSELF RUN OVER BY THE TRAIN
JAN · 11 · 1878

HARRY SISLEY OF
KILBURN AGED 10
DROWNED IN ATTEMPTING
TO SAVE HIS BROTHER
AFTER HE HIMSELF HAD
JUST BEEN RESCUED
MAY · 24 · 1878

JAMES HEWERS
ON SEPT · 24 · 1878
WAS KILLED BY A TRAIN
AT RICHMOND IN THE
ENDEAVOUR TO SAVE
ANOTHER MAN

GEORGE BLENCOWE
AGED 16
WHEN A FRIEND BATHING IN
THE LEA CRIED FOR HELP
WENT TO HIS RESCUE
AND WAS DROWNED
SEPT · 6 · 1880

St Botolph, Aldersgate Churchyard. Panel from the National Memorial
to heroic men and women.

Forgotten Stones. St Pancras Old Churchyard.

It is a pleasant little garden with trees, flowerbeds and a row of seats. The garden is well protected by the north wall and faces south so that in good weather the seats are sunny and warm.

ALL HALLOWS, STAINING, MARK LANE EC3

All that remains of this church and its churchyard is a small enclosure on the west side of Mark Lane, on which stands the parish hall of St Olave's (the two parishes having been united) and the old tower of the church.

ST ALPHAGE, LONDON WALL EC2

This is one of the older City churchyards. St Alphage, Archbishop of Canterbury in 1006, was murdered by the Danes in 1012. The first church, built shortly after this, along the inner side of the City wall adjoining Cripplegate, was dedicated to him. The churchyard extended eastwards along the wall, probably as far as the postern in the wall at Aldermanbury. The church fell into disrepair and was pulled down in 1536 and thereupon the City Corporation claimed that the site of the church reverted to it as 'soil of the city'. It seems clear however that they allowed the old churchyard to continue in use. After the dissolution of the monasteries the parish took over part of the chapel of the priory hospital of St Mary the Virgin lying to the south-east. All that remains today is the ruin of the fourteenth-century tower of the chapel.

The churchyard, which is approached from Wood Street via St Alphage Gardens, is now a well-stocked garden, neatly laid out. A portion of the old City wall runs through it. It bears a notice that the churchyard was closed in 1853 and laid out as a garden in 1872. The garden on the north side of the wall was not part of the churchyard, despite the fact that its flowerbeds are cruciform in shape; this was acquired as part of the re-development of the area following the extensive war damage. The two sides of the garden can accommodate a number of people and being well sheltered and facing south they are much patronized in summertime.

25

18th century burial-ground of St Andrew, Holborn.

ST ANDREW, HOLBORN EC2

This church stands at the south-east corner of Holborn Circus at the junction of Holborn and St Andrew's Street. It is now below street level, but when built it was well placed on a hill above the valley of the river Fleet. It is the largest parish church built by Wren, and until the nineteenth century served one of the biggest parishes in London.

Not much of the original churchyard remains. A substantial part of the north portion was lost when the Viaduct was built in 1863, and the whole of the southern part was taken in 1870 for the building of a new rectory and Court House. What remains provides two small gardens; one is the church garden along the north wall through which one enters the church from Holborn Viaduct; the other, maintained by the City Corporation, is at the west end of the church. From the latter one should note the two figures of charity children, which have been placed on the west front of the tower; these were originally outside the parish school in Hatton Garden built by Wren's master mason Mark Strong in 1696. From the church garden one sees on the north wall the Resurrection Stone, depicting the Last Judgement with many small bodies climbing out of their tombs. This stone was originally over the entrance to the paupers' burial-ground in Shoe Lane, itself now buried beneath the site of Farringdon Street.

The churchyard has other charitable associations. A memorial tablet inside the church, erected by the Worshipful Company of Cordwainers, commemorates:

'William Marsden
1796 M.D. Surgeon 1867.'

who, 'as a result of finding a young woman dying on the steps of the churchyard on a winter's night in 1827', founded in 1828 The Royal Free Hospital for Women, which until 1974 stood in Gray's Inn Road.

The church also contains the tomb of Thomas Coram 'Master Mariner, Colonial Administrator, and Philanthropist, died 28th March 1751 aged 83, who founded the Foundlings Hospital 20th November 1739'. He was not buried here, but in the chapel of the Hospital in Lamb's Conduit Fields. However when the church was restored in 1961 after the war damage, his tomb, together with the pulpit, font and organ, was transferred from the Foundling Hospital, which had meanwhile emigrated to Berkhamstead. This was entirely appropriate because the original foundling hospital was opened by Coram in a house in Hatton Garden within the parish in 1741.

Amongst those buried here were the Elizabethan John Webster, author of *The White Devil* and *The Duchess of Malfi*, who may at one time have been the parish clerk (died 1625); Dr Henry Sachaverell, who was made Rector in 1713 as a reward for his tribulations and trial for seditious libel as a result of his outspoken preaching (died 1724); and Charles Lamb's parents and his aunt Sarah Lamb (Aunt Hetty of *The Essays of Elia*) (died 1797). Here too was buried Thomas Baron Wriothesley, Lord Chancellor and subsequently Earl of Southampton (died 1550), to whom Henry VIII gave large estates which became available from the dissolution of the monasteries, including properties at Beaulieu, Stratton Micheldever and Titchfield, as well as the manors of Bloomsbury and St Giles in London and the advowson of St Andrew's.

The burial of the poet Thomas Chatterton (died 1770) is also recorded at the age of seventeen, but as he took his own life his body was interred in the paupers' burial-ground in Shoe Lane.

✿ ST ANDREW'S GARDENS, GRAY'S INN ROAD WC1

Like so many churches in the eighteenth century St Andrew, Holborn found that its churchyard was not big enough and a new burial-ground was acquired in Gray's Inn Road in 1754, on the east side of the road, a little to the south of the land on which William Marsden built his hospital. After its closure as a burial-ground it was reopened as a public garden, known as St Andrew's Gardens, on 29 July 1885 by Lady John Manners. It is now maintained by Camden Council. It is not of great interest but it covers a large area and makes a good garden with plenty of grass, flower-beds and trees. A few of the larger tombs have been left in position but in the main the gravestones, which are mostly of the early nineteenth century, have been placed along the boundaries.

All that is left of this churchyard is a very small garden on the north side of the church, which is entered from St Mary Axe. This contains a few gravestones and two memorial seats – one to Mrs Frances Godfree, parishioner 1925–51, and the other to George Kimberley Perkins 1957–74. The only stone which one can read is a memorial to Mary Datchelor (died 1725) and her two sisters. Mary was a generous benefactor of the parish and the stone records: 'Beneath is the original stone of Mary Datchelor whose munificent gift to this parish founded the Mary Datchelor girls school at Camberwell. Let her own works praise her. Prov. xxxi 31.'

This is the church and burial place of John Stow (died 1605), to whose great *Survey of London* all interested in the history of the City are immeasurably indebted. Others to be buried here were Philip Malpas, sheriff in 1439, who 'at his decease gave one hundred and twenty pounds to poor prisioners, and every year for five years four hundred and three shirts and smocks, forty pairs of sheets, and one hundred and fifty gowns of frieze to the poor, to poor maids marriages one hundred marks, to highways one hundred marks, and to five hundred poor people in London every one six shillings and eight pence, etc'; Sir Thomas Offley (died 1582), merchant taylor, Lord Mayor 1556, who, says Stow, writing as a parishioner, 'bequeathed the one half of his goods to charitable actions, but the parish received little benefit thereby'; and William Wight (died 1672), an uncle of Samuel Pepys, about whom the following entry appears in Pepys's Diary on 11 May 1664:

'My uncle Wight . . . and from me went to my house to see my wife; and strange to think that my wife should by and by send for me after he was gone, to tell me that he should begin discourse of her want of children and his also, and how he thought it would be best for him and her to have one between them, and he would give her £500 in money or jewels beforehand and make the child his heyre. He commended her body and discoursed that for all he knew the thing was lawful. She says she did give him a very warm answer, such as he did excuse himself by saying

28

that he said this in jest but told her that since he saw what her mind was, he would say no more to her of it, and desired her to make no word of it. It seemed he did say all of this in a kind of counterfeit laugh; but by all words that passed, which I cannot now so well set down, it is plain to me that he was in good earnest, and that I fear all his kindness is but his lust for her. What to think of it of a sudden I know not, but I think not to take notice yet of it to him till I have thought better of it. So, with my mind and head a little troubled . . .'

His tomb was discovered during restoration work in 1930 and bears the following inscription:

> 'Stay Courteous Reader spend a teare
> Uppon the dust that slumbers here
> And whilst thou Readest ye state of mee
> Think on the glasse that runs for thee.'

✠ ST ANDREW–BY–THE–WARDROBE, QUEEN VICTORIA STREET EC4

The main entrance to this church was originally on its north side from St Andrew's Hill, and a very small portion of the churchyard remains here as a paved garden with a few seats and floral containers. On the construction of Queen Victoria Street in 1871 the south side of the church was opened up and a more imposing doorway with steps down to an excellent pair of entrance gates on the new street was made. In 1901 what remained of the southern side of the churchyard was made into a terraced garden. For those who do not mind the roar of the traffic there are here plenty of seats in the sun.

✠ ST ANNE AND ST AGNES, GRESHAM STREET EC2

Here there is a good small garden. It is also an unusual one in that it has grown larger, instead of smaller, since it was a churchyard. When Noble

Street was widened after the 1939–45 War the City Corporation took the opportunity of extending the garden on the east side so that there is now a good stone terrace on the Noble Street side with plenty of seats backed by flowerbeds, grass and trees. The garden continues along the south side of the church, but there are no seats within this, the old churchyard, area, which retains a few tombstones, including that of Samuel Barber, plumber, died 1819.

The attractive red-brick Wren church, which is tucked away in the north-west corner of the plot, is small, almost domestic, and provides an harmonious background to the green of the garden. In Stow's time the church had the delightful name of St Anne-in-the-Willows, so called, he says, 'I know not upon what occasion, but some say of willows growing thereabouts, but now there is no such void place for willows to grow, more than the churchyard, where do grow some high ash trees.'

Here was buried Peter Heiwood (died 1701) who, according to his memorial in the church, 'apprehended Guy Faux with his dark lanthorn; and for his zealous prosecution of Papists as Justice of Peace was stabbed in Westminster Hall by John James a Dominican Friar AD 1640'. The epitaph concluding:

> 'Reader, if not a papist bred
> Upon such ashes gently tread.'

ST ANNE, BLACKFRIARS EC4

The church of St Anne, Blackfriars, which had only been built in 1597, was destroyed in the Great Fire and not rebuilt, but its site and its church-yard continued to be used as places of burial until 1849. In 1964 the City Corporation assumed responsibility for their upkeep as gardens.

This area took its name from the Black Friars – the Dominicans – who moved here from their original house in Holborn in 1278 and who soon built up a large establishment. Their great priory church covered an area between what are now Blackfriars Lane to the west and Friary Street to the east. As Stow says, 'this was a large church, and richly furnished with ornaments, wherin divers parliaments and other great meetings, hath been holden'. Here it was that, in 1529, Cardinal Wolsey was condemned 'in the praemunire', that is to say, for asserting papal jurisdiction in England.

The little lane known today as Church Entry marks the site of the passage from north to south between the chancel and the nave. South of this, with an entrance in Ireland Yard, stood the Provincial's Hall.

After the priory submitted to Henry VIII the main priory buildings (including the parish church which the friars had provided for people living within the priory precincts) were given, in 1550, to Sir Thomas Cawarden, who demolished the greater part of them. In 1597, no doubt in reparation for having pulled down the old parish church, he built a new parish church – St Anne's – in Ireland Yard on the site of the Provincial's Hall. At the same time a portion of the land to the north which had formed part of the old nave was allocated as a churchyard.

Approaching from Ludgate Hill one comes first to the old churchyard, which is reached by turning left out of the Broadway into Carter's Lane and then right into Church Entry. Here is the old churchyard. Church Entry leads down to Ireland Lane on the left where there is the second garden on the old church site. Both gardens are charming and compact, secluded and remarkably quiet. Each is enclosed on three sides by office buildings, the church garden being open to the south and the churchyard to the east – its open side being protected by a brick wall, railings and a gate. The Church Entry garden is the more attractive. It is paved and has a very fine ailanthus tree – the 'Tree of Heaven' – in the centre and plenty of seats. There are tombstones round the walls and also some in the northern paving of the garden. The stones on the west side were removed from the churchyard of St Peter, Paul's Wharf when that site was acquired by the City Corporation in 1960. Those on the north side were moved from the churchyard of St Mary Somerset when Upper Thames Street was widened in 1968. The garden in Ireland Yard has the advantage of facing south but is the more exposed. It contains the only remaining fragment of the old priory buildings – a portion of the south wall of the Provincial's Hall.

Stow lists the names of many distinguished people buried in the old priory church, including Margaret Queen of Scots, transferred from the original priory church in Holborn; Sir John Triptoste, Earl of Worcester, beheaded in 1470; James Tuochet, Lord Dudley, beheaded in 1497; and also 'the heart of Queen Helianor, the foundress, the heart of Alfonce her son and the hearts of John and Margaret the children of W. Valence'.

The new church being close to the Elizabethan Blackfriars Theatre, which was constructed out of another part of the priory, had theatrical associations. (Shakespeare is known to have bought a house in Ireland Yard.) In the new church the Shakespearean actor Nathaniel Field (died 1633) was buried, as were Helen, daughter of Richard Burbage, the great tragedian, who managed the theatre, Isaac Oliver (died 1617), one of Britain's greatest miniaturists and the famous engraver William Faithorne (died 1691).

ST ANNE, SOHO, SHAFTESBURY AVENUE W1

St Anne, Soho, one of the three churches outside the City attributed to Wren, was built in 1686 to serve the new development then taking place in Soho. At that time Shaftesbury Avenue, a creation of the nineteenth century, did not exist and Dean Street and Wardour Street (then known as So Ho) were only partially built up, the entrance to the church being from what was then called King Street. The dedication was in honour of Anne Princess of Denmark, subsequently Queen of England.

Wren's church was destroyed by enemy action in the 1939–45 War and has not been rebuilt. Only the tower, which had been added in 1801–3, survived, together with the churchyard. The churchyard is now a green garden and the tower, which has been described as 'the greatest originality in church architecture probably displayed' in the nineteenth century, forms the delightful central feature of its terrace background. The tower carries two tablets to mark its first two centenaries and also a number of commemorative tablets, the most recent being that of Dorothy L. Sayers, writer of detective stories and theologian, who was a churchwarden here until her death in 1957 and whose ashes are buried here.

The most famous person to be buried here was William Hazlitt, who died at No. 6 Frith Street, and for whom a gravestone has been left in the north side of the grass lawn, although his original stone, which bore a lengthy inscription, was removed in 1870. His tablet on the tower reads:

'On the northern side of this ground lie the remains of
William Hazlitt, painter, critic, essayist.

Born Maidstone April 10 1778.
Died Soho September 18 1830.
Restored by his grandson 1901.'

Another tablet records the death and burial of Theodore King of Corsica
in the following lines:

'Near this place is interred
Theodore King of Corsica
Who died in this parish Decr. 11 1756
Immediately after leaving the King's Bench Prison
By the benefit of the Act of Insolvency
In consequence of which he registered his Kingdom of Corsica
For the use of his creditors.

The Grave, Great Teacher, to a Level Brings,
Heroes and Beggars Galley-slaves and Kings.
But Theodore his Moral Learned Ere Dead
Fate poured its Lessons on his Living Head
Bestow'd a Kingdom and Denied Him Bread.'

These lines are said to have been written by Horace Walpole. It is also
said that the King was saved from a pauper's grave by John Wright, an
oilman who lived in Compton Street, who announced that 'for once he
was willing to pay the funeral expenses of a King'.

St Anne's claimed to be the first parish to elect a Burial Board under
the provisions of the Burial Act of 1852. It met in July 1854 and in 1855
acquired two acres of ground in the London Necropolis Company
Cemetery for the use of the parish and thereafter burials in the churchyard
ceased. In 1869 the boundary wall along Wardour Street was rebuilt at
a lower height and an entrance opened in it. At the same time a number
of tombstones were removed and the churchyard tidied up. In 1891 the
care of the churchyard was taken over by the Metropolitan Gardens Association but it is now maintained by the local authority.

Today access is from Wardour Street only. The Shaftesbury Avenue
entrance has been closed and it is no longer possible to reach the churchyard
from the site of the church which is used as a car park.

✠ ST BARTHOLOMEW THE GREAT, SMITHFIELD EC1

One enters this churchyard from West Smithfield through a fine piece of Elizabethan domestic architecture (1595) in which is set a Gothic arch, originally the entrance to the south aisle of the church. It was in the square in front of this building that the martyrs were burnt, or boiled, to death. In 1546 Lord Chancellor Wriothesley, the Duke of Norfolk, the Earl of Bradford and the Lord Mayor sat on a bench outside the west door, to watch four persons die at the stake.

The present churchyard was only made in the sixteenth century after the dissolution of the monasteries. The Augustinian Priory, founded by Rahere in 1123, was surrendered to the Crown in 1539. At this time the church extended as far as the entrance already mentioned and the burial-ground provided for the parish was on the north side of the church. Very soon after the surrender the north transept and the whole of the nave were pulled down. This provided not only valuable materials for sale but also building land. In 1544 all the land within the monastic walls was sold to Sir Richard Rich for £1064 11s 3d. The grant in his favour provided that what remained of the monastic church should thereafter become the parish church and that 'all the vacant land and soil containing in length eighty-seven feet of assize and in breadth sixty feet next adjacent to the said parish church of St Bartholomew the Apostle the Great aforesaid as is before mentioned by us prepared on the west side of the same church shall be for the future received and reputed for the burying-place of the said parish church . . .'

This left him free to develop the western part of the old nave as well as the earlier burial-ground which adjoined the land – also monastic property – on which the Great Fair took place. This Fair, held at the time of the Feast of St Bartholomew (24 August) since before the foundation of the Priory, continued until 1854.

Medieval records show that in the fourteenth century the sacrist of the monastery was allowed to collect (and keep) rent for grazing in the church-yard and stallage for cattle stalls provided by him for the Fair both inside and outside the church.

It was in this older churchyard too that on the Eve of St Bartholomew's Day the schoolboys of London used to come, as Stow tells us, to dispute about the principles of grammar:

> '... for I myself,' he writes, 'in my youth, have yearly seen, on the eve of St Bartholomew the Apostle, the scholars of divers grammar schools repair unto the churchyard of St Bartholomew, the priory in Smithfield, where upon a bank boarded about under a tree, some one scholar hath stepped up, and there hath opposed and answered, till he were by some better scholar overcome and put down; and the overcomer taking the place, did like as the first; and in the end the best opposers and answerers had rewards, which I observe not but it made both good schoolmasters, and also good scholars, diligently against such times to prepare them-selves for the obtaining of this garland.'

In the new churchyard there was introduced in the seventeenth century a practice of distributing on each Good Friday morning the sum of ten shillings amongst poor widows of the parish. In 1888 the distribution was changed to 20 sixpences and buns for children, and this came to be known as the 'Good Friday sixpences'. The custom is still observed today in the gift of 'hot cross buns' in the churchyard on Good Friday mornings after the church service.

With such a magnificent church as this it is not surprising that many famous people were buried here. These included, in addition to Rahere, its founder (died 1144): Dr Richard Bartlett, President of the Royal College of Physicians and doctor to Henry VIII (died 1558); Sir Richard Rich, who bought the monastic lands, became Lord Chancellor as Lord Rich and founded Felsted School (died 1567); Sir Walter Mildmay (died 1589) and his wife Mary (died 1576), he was Chancellor of the Exchequer and founded

Emmanuel College, Cambridge; and Thomas Roycroft (died 1677), King's Printer in Eastern languages and publisher of the Polyglot Bible.

⚜ ST BENET FINK, THREADNEEDLE STREET EC2

This is a very small garden which it is easy to overlook. It is just behind the Royal Exchange, lying between the statue of George Peabody, the American philanthropist, and No. 1 Threadneedle Street. The garden marks the site of the church, which was pulled down in 1842 to make room for the new Royal Exchange. Its former churchyard, in which the statue was erected in 1869, lay to the west.

The shape of the site, on which a church stood for over six hundred years, is interesting. The church, destroyed in the Great Fire, was rebuilt by Wren and was considered to be one of his more felicitous achievements – a ten-sided church to match the site.

Its peculiar name, according to Stow, is derived from its founder, who also gave his name to Finch Lane, then called Finke's Lane.

⚜ ST BENET SHEREHOG, PANCRAS LANE EC4

This church was destroyed in the Great Fire and not rebuilt. All that remains today is some boundary stones, erected in 1892, and a City Corporation plaque. It affords some idea of what the disused churchyards must have looked like a century ago.

This church too is thought to derive its peculiar name from a benefactor.

⚜ ST BOTOLPH, ALDERSGATE EC1

St Botolph was the patron saint of travellers and there were four City churches near its gates dedicated to him. Three survive today; the fourth,

St Botolph, Billingsgate, was not rebuilt after the Great Fire.

This garden, which is on the south side of the church and can be approached from either Aldersgate Street or King Edward Street, is the second largest in the City – exceeded in size only by Finsbury Circus. It comprises the churchyards of St Botolph and of St Leonard, Foster Lane (which was not rebuilt after the Great Fire; it stood where the General Post Office building now stands) and the burial-ground of Christchurch, Newgate Street. Some further land was added after its opening as a garden in 1880. From its position it is generally known as 'Postman's Park'.

The association with the Post Office remains. One of the seats in the garden bears a plaque reading:

> 'This seat was given by Mr Hill in gratitude for the hours he was able to rest in Postman's Park in between his duties as a City postman and as a thanksgiving for his safe return from his 3 years in France with his regiment the 8th City of London Post Office Rifles and especially in remembrance of the 2000 of the Regiment killed there.'

There is also a tree planted by Sir William Ryland, Chairman of the Post Office, on 26 February 1973, to mark the issue of the first postage stamp featuring a tree.

On the north-west wall of the garden is a National Memorial to heroic men and women who gave their lives attempting to save the lives of others. It was the idea of the painter G. F. Watts, conceived by him at the time of Queen Victoria's Golden Jubilee in 1887, although the Memorial was not dedicated until 1900. It contains in the centre a small statuette of Mr Watts and on either side are the plaques recording a number of acts of gallantry by men, women and children. The plaques are sheltered by a loggia with seats underneath. There are now some fifty plaques but none have been added since 1928.

The earliest tablet commemorates:

> 'Sarah Smith, Pantomime Artiste at Prince's Theatre, who died of horrible injuries received when attempting in her inflammable dress to extinguish the flames which had enveloped her companion. January 24th 1863.'

Another tablet records the death by drowning of John Cranmer Cambridge, a London County Council employee, and reads:

> 'John Cranmer Cambridge aged 23 a clerk in the London County Council who was drowned near Ostend whilst saving the life of a stranger and foreigner, August 8th 1901.'

The latest of the tablets commemorates Police Constable Edwin Cook of the Metropolitan Police who gave his life on 7 October 1927.

Sir John Micklethwait, physician to Charles II and President of the Royal College of Physicians (died 1683), was buried at St Botolph's. In St Leonard's Stow mentions the monument of John Brokeitwell, who might well have been a demolition man but is described as 'an especial re-edifier, or new builder thereof'.

The garden is a spacious and welcoming one with plenty of seats, some of which have been given as memorials. There is a sundial, a pleasant fountain, a good modern statue of the Minotaur by Michael Ayrton, some excellent trees and plenty of grass and flowerbeds.

Outside the garden by the Aldersgate Street entrance is a plaque erected on 24 May 1926 by the International Methodist Historical Union to commemorate the conversion of John and Charles Wesley in May 1738, this being the spot where John Wesley felt his heart 'strangely warmed'.

ST BOTOLPH, ALDGATE EC3

> 'From Aldgate east,' wrote Stow, 'lieth a large street and highway, sometimes replenished with few, but fair and comely buildings; on the north side whereof, the first was the parish church of St Botolph, in a large cemetery or churchyard.'

The original churchyard extended some way north of the church, but today there remains only a fringe bordering the church on the north, west and south sides. The church is unusual in facing north instead of east; the porch and baptistry are at the south end. Here there is an enclosed space containing two good plane trees and some seats: on the outer wall is a drinking fountain commemorating Frederic David Mocatta – dated 16 January 1905.

On the west side there remain a number of tombstones. One is that of Wyeth Canwarden, Wine Cooper, who died 15 November 1765, aged sixty-five; another is that of Thomas Ebrall, Citizen and Corn Merchant, 'who was shot by a Life Guardsman on the 9th April 1810 in the shop of Mr Goodeve Fenchurch Street and died on the 17th day of the said month in the 24th year of his life'.

It was not long after his untimely death that another tragedy occurred in this churchyard. As reported in the *Weekly Dispatch* of 9 September 1838, a gravedigger, Thomas Oates and a young fish dealer, Edward Luddett, who went to his assistance, died from the noxious fumes arising from a paupers' grave into which the gravedigger had descended. (A paupers' grave was a deep grave kept open until filled; which meant that some seventeen or eighteen bodies would be buried in it.) At the inquest the Deputy of the Ward said that on several occasions he had sent a present-ment to the Archdeacon of the Diocese or his Surrogate, 'descriptive of the filthy state of the vaults and burial-ground, but that no notice had been taken of the evil'.

Amongst others to be buried here were Lord Darcy, who was beheaded on nearby Tower Hill in 1537 for plotting against Henry VIII; Sir Nicholas Carew, who suffered a similar fate for the same reason in 1538; Robert Dow (died 1612), Merchant Taylor and philanthropist, who left money to the parish and to Christ's Hospital and also to St Sepulchre's church 'for ringing the greatest bell on the day the condemned prisoners [in Newgate gaol] are executed' and 'for other services for ever concerning such condemned prisoners'; Alderman Sir John Cass (died 1718) who founded the school which stands on the opposite side of Houndsditch; and William Symington (died 1831) who invented the first steamboat. In addi-tion, over five thousand nameless victims of the Great Plague of 1665 were buried here in two communal graves.

ST BOTOLPH, BISHOPSGATE EC2

St Botolph, Bishopsgate stood just outside the City walls on the main road leading north. It is thought that there was a church on this site before the Norman Conquest. Stow describes it as being 'in a fair churchyard, adjoining to the town ditch, upon the very bank thereof, but of old time enclosed with a comely wall of brick, lately repaired by Sir William Allen, mayor in the year 1571, because he was born in that parish where also he was buried'. The churchyard was on the south side of the church and, as he says, stretched right down to the ditch. It was enlarged in 1615 and again in 1760.

Fortunately more of the churchyard than usual has survived and the garden which has been created is one of the finest in the City. One or two gravestones remain and there is a good tomb of Sir William Rawlins Kt who died on 26 March 1838 aged eighty-five. He had been sheriff in 1801 and was an upholsterer by trade, having had as one of his apprentices Thomas Dibdin, the illegitimate son of Charles Dibdin, author of 'Tom Bowling' (who is buried in St James's burial-ground, Camden Town). The garden also contains the War Memorial Cross of the Honourable Artillery Company. Part of the garden is now laid out as a tennis court, and there are plenty of seats and flowerbeds. To the west of the church is a charming red-brick building (formerly a school, now a hall) which blends well with the red brick of the eighteenth-century church. A tablet over the door records that it was built in 1861 and restored in 1952 by the Worshipful Company of Fanmakers, who now use it as their Hall. In two niches flanking the door stand the figures of two children in eighteenth-century dress, a boy who bears the number 18 and a girl the number 25. These figures, which date from 1821, were originally on the former school building in Peter Street.

This garden is interesting too because we know something of the story of its transformation from a disused churchyard. The Rev William Rogers, Rector from 1863 to 1896, was a remarkable man, a great social reformer and educationalist. In 1888 he published his entertaining *Reminiscences*. In these he wrote:

'Our churchyard, when I came here, was a dirty unwholesome spot, and a receptacle for all the dead cats and dogs and offal of the neighbourhood. I was very anxious to remove the nuisance, but it was hard to see how. At last an opportunity presented itself in the shape of a vigorous churchwarden with country ideas and aesthetical tastes. We decided to turn the place into a garden.

St Botolph, Bishopsgate. Church Hall and tomb of Sir William Rawlins.

HERE

LIES THE BODY OF
Mʳˢ SUSANNA WESLEY,
widow of the Rev. Samuel Wesley, M.A.
late Rector of Epworth in Lincolnshire,
who died July 23. 1742,
aged 73 years.

She was the youngest daughter of the
Rev. Samuel Annesley D.D. ejected by the Act
of uniformity from the Rectory of Sᵗ Giles's
Cripplegate, Aug. 24. 1662.

She was the Mother of nineteen Children
of whom the most eminent were the
REVS. JOHN AND CHARLES WESLEY,
the former of whom was under God the
Founder of the Societies of the People
called Methodists.

In sure and certain hope to rise
and claim her mansion in the skies,
a Christian here her flesh laid down,
the Cross exchanging for a Crown.

Above: Bunhill Fields Burial-ground 1866.
Left: Tombstone of Mrs Susanna Wesley, Bunhill Fields.
Right: Bunhill Fields to-day with the tomb of Joseph Denison.

Chelsea Old Church before the construction of the Embankment (c.1799).

Open spaces are all the fashion now, and it looks as if before long every old burial-ground in London will be turned into a place of recreation. Those who do not remember it will hardly credit the outcry that was raised twenty years ago when our intentions became known. A section of the press was shocked at my sacrilege, and the parishioners were up in arms. Many tombstones had to be removed and to hide the operations from the vulgar gaze a tarpaulin was put up. Nothing would persuade the public that the vilest practices were not being perpetrated. People waxed indignant at the violence which was being done to the bones of their ancestors, and the Rectory front door was besieged by heartbroken descendants.

'I could endure it no further, and consulted the churchwarden. "Send them all to me and I will settle with them", he said. So I did. When an individual appeared and began in sepulchral style to harangue me, I cut him short by saying that if his troubles were spiritual, I should be happy to assist him in grappling with them, but that if he had come about the bones of his ancestors, I begged to refer him to the churchwarden. That gentleman proved equal to the situation. He insisted upon a glass of wine, perhaps two, being regarded as a preliminary to the discussion of all grievances connected with the project, and the malcontents rarely resisted. And as the churchwarden afterwards triumphantly remarked "a dozen of sherry at 30s. squared the lot of them". I need hardly say however that everything was done decently and in order, and we offered to put a tablet in the church in memory of any person whose bones could be satisfactorily identified.

'The garden at once became very popular, and it continues to be one of the brightest spots in the City of London. We started a sort of "Zoo" in connection with it, notably two Royal cygnets, a pair of peacocks presented by the late Baroness Rothschild, and several storks which Lord Reay imported from Holland. I was on the look-out for a bear when it became necessary to disband the menagerie. The screams of the peacocks disturbed the devotions of the congregation, London smoke spoiled the appearance of the storks. At present our modest aviary is restricted to a few pheasants which the parish beadle is fattening for Christmas.'

In his book he also noted the curious habit of earlier registrars recording the deaths of those buried here by nickname or description, as, for example: 'Onlye Toolarge, Milksoppe, Fortune Hunt, and "Henry Hardup that died in the Cage" [a reference to the small prison on old London Bridge], and "Charles Jones and Hance Gotman the one slew the other in fight".'

Others to be buried here included Sir William Allen, mercer, Lord Mayor 1571; 'Lady Mary Bohun, alias Stafford, buried out of Bethlehem house, aged 140 years' (died 1608); Sir Paul Pindar, His Majesty's Ambassador to the Turkish Emperor 1611 and 'nine years resident' (died 1650 aged eighty-four), the façade of whose fine house in Bishopsgate is still to be seen in the Victoria and Albert Museum; and the great Puritan John Lilburne (died 1657). Another remarkable man buried here was the former Rector John Lake, who was inducted in 1663, and who subsequently became first Bishop of Sodor and Man, then of Bristol and finally of Chichester (from which see he retired on the accession of William and Mary, refusing to take the oath of allegiance and supremacy). He fought on the side of the Royalists in the Civil War and remained in the Army for four years after being ordained. He also took part, when Bishop of Bristol, in the campaign against the Monmouth rebels.

🦁 ST BRIDE, FLEET STREET EC4

The present church stands on a raised plateau surrounded by its former churchyard. In the crypt are the remains of a Roman pavement and it is possible that this was a Roman place of burial. The excavations carried out when the church was restored after the heavy damage suffered in the 1939–45 War have disclosed the remains of both Saxon and Norman churches.

The south side of the old churchyard is now the garden of the rectory but the remainder is open to the public. It lies well back from both Fleet Street and New Bridge Street and is surprisingly quiet and secluded. It is the best spot from which to admire Wren's magnificent steeple – completed in 1703. It is a paved garden well shaded by its trees and with plenty of seats. A number of tombstones remain dating mainly from the seventeenth century to the early nineteenth. Some now form part of the paving. Immediately inside the entrance gates on the left is the vault of the Holden family dated 1657. They were hatters in Fleet Street, Samuel Pepys being one of their customers. Another stone which is still legible is that of the Evans family. It reads:

> 'In memory of Mr George Evans of this parish Victualler, who died 8th September 1766 aged 61 years; and Susannah Evans his wife. She died 21st October 1777 aged 62 years; and George Evans their son, Many years an Apothecary of Holborn Bridge. He died 17th February 1816 aged 62 years.'

The entrance gates are a memorial to Valentine Knapp – President of the Newspaper Society 1919–22, and were erected by the Society in 1956. There is also a memorial seat to 'Paul Einzig Author and Economist 1897–1973'.

Also buried here were Wynkyn de Worde (died 1534) who succeeded to Caxton's business as a printer and whose premises were just opposite the church. He was the first to print music in England. Thomas Weelkes the madrigalist (died 1623); Sir Richard Baker, author of *The Chronicles of the Kings of England*, who died 1645 imprisoned in the nearby Fleet prison for debt; Richard Lovelace the Cavalier poet (died 1658); Thomas Pepys, the brother of Samuel (died 1664); and Samuel Richardson, the first English novelist, who started in Fleet Street as a printer (died 1761).

Writing of his brother's funeral in his diary on 18 March 1664 Pepys vividly illustrates the difficulties of interment within the church, which were to become such a scandal in the nineteenth century. In his words:

> '... and to the church and with the grave-maker chose a place for my brother to lie in, just under my mother's pew. But to see how a man's tombes are at the mercy of such a fellow, that for 6d. he would (as his own words were) "I will justle them together but I will make room for him" – speaking of the fullness of the middle Isle where he was to lie. And that he would for my father's sake do my brother that is dead all the civility he can; which was to disturb other corpses that are not quite rotten

to make room for him. And me thought his manner of speaking it was very remarkable – as of a thing that now was in his power to do a man a courtesy or not.'

🦎 BUNHILL FIELDS, CITY ROAD EC1

Bunhill Fields burial-ground lies in Finsbury, a little way outside the old City walls, on the west side of City Road to the north of the 'Artillery Ground' of the Honourable Artillery Company and opposite John Wesley's old home, chapel and grave.

From the seventeenth century Bunhill Fields became for the Dissenting dead what St Paul's was for the members of the Established Church, their *Campo Santo*, as Southey described it. Few, if any, of the Nonconformist chapels and meeting places in the City had their own burial-grounds, and Bunhill Fields, which as far as is known was never consecrated, was the only place within reach where they could bury their dead without the ministration of an Anglican priest. In consequence the majority of the great Nonconformist poets, writers, scholars and divines, amongst them many of our best-known hymnologists, lie here.

The story of the Fields however goes back far beyond the seventeenth century. It has been suggested that the name Bunhill Fields is a corruption of Bone-hill Fields and that there was a burial-ground in this vicinity in Saxon times. Being outside the City walls many things could be done in the fields which could not within the City. Here the apprentices could sport themselves, archers could practise and the trained bands could drill. In the earliest map of London published in about 1555 archers are shown in various postures in Fynnesburie Field on the site of what came to be known in later maps as the 'Artillery Ground'.

The site of the burial-ground is believed to have formed part of a prebendal estate belonging to St Paul's Cathedral, but it did not become a place of regular burial until the seventeenth century. In 1315 the City was granted a lease at a rent of 20 shillings a year. This lease was renewed in 1553 for a term of 90 years at an annual rent of £29 13s 4d. Then in 1561 the lease was extended for a further 140 years in return for the City providing some twenty tons of lead for the repair of the cathedral roof which had been severely damaged by a terrible storm which ravaged the City in that year.

In 1549 the charnel chapel of St Paul's was pulled down and the bones taken from it were buried in Bunhill Fields, then still known as Finsbury Field; but it was not until 1665 that it became recognized as a place of burial. Daniel Defoe suggested that it was used as one of the pits for the burial of victims of the Great Plague of that year, but this view is now discounted. In Maitland's *Survey of London*, published in 1739, he writes:

> 'Part of Bunhill Fields, at present denominated Tindal's, or the Dissenters' great Burial Ground, was, by the Mayor and Citizens of London, in the year 1665, set apart and consecrated as a common cemetery, for the interment of such corpses as could not have room in their own parochial burial-grounds in that dreadful year of pestilence. However, it not being made use of on that occasion, the said Tindal took a lease thereof, and converted it into a burial-ground for the use of Dissenters.'

For some time the burial-ground bore the name of its lessee. It passed from Tindal to James Browne and then to Elizabeth Fetherstonhaugh, but by about 1741 it had reverted to the City Corporation.

The burial-ground was enlarged in 1700 to cover about five acres. It is recorded that at the time of its closure in 1853 some 120,000 burials had taken place in the grounds.

In 1865 the Court of Common Council resolved that:

> 'considering the high historic interest attaching to the Bunhill Fields Burial Ground, in consequence of the interment of so many distinguished and honourable men of all creeds and parties, this Court is willing to accept the care and preservation of the ground on behalf of the public, and to assist in promoting any well-advised scheme for securing against molestation and disturbance the final resting-place of so many of their fellow citizens.'

In 1867 an Act of Parliament was passed providing that the burial-ground should at all times be kept as an open space accessible to the public under the control of the City Corporation. Bunhill Fields was opened to the public as Gardens in 1869 after, in the words of the Chairman:

'Tombs have been raised from beneath the ground, stones have been set straight, illegible inscriptions have been deciphered and re-cut, hundreds of decayed tombs have been restored, paths have been laid and avenues planted.'

It was at this time that the present gate and railings, with their inscriptions, in City Road, were erected.

The gardens did not escape the bombs of the 1939–45 War, the greatest damage being done in the northern section.

In 1950 the monuments and boundary walls were listed by the Ministry of Town and Country Planning as of architectural and historic interest. At the same time consideration was given to the future of the burial-ground. It was decided that, as the northern part had suffered the greatest damage, that area should be cleared of monuments and laid out simply as a garden, and at the same time the other tombs should be railed off from the paths leading through the burial-ground. These improvements were completed in 1965 at a cost of approximately £55,000.

The plane trees, which themselves are getting on in years, the shrubs and green grass, the footpaths and the seats, all combine to put this spot high amongst the green oases to be found in the City area, and the northern garden in summer is a particular success. Bunhill Fields however still remains one of the burial-grounds where a good deal of interest attaches to the names of those who were buried here.

There is room to mention only a few of them, but those who would wish for more detailed information are referred to the two volumes entitled *Bunhill Fields* published by the late Alfred Light, the first in 1913 and the second in 1933, which contain over 150 short biographical notes relating to the graves which he was able to identify positively. In addition the Guildhall Library contains a copy of every inscription which was legible when the City Corporation took over in 1865. Today an interesting little Corporation Guide can be bought at the kiosk in the middle of the garden.

In the nineteenth century new monuments were erected to commemorate the most famous of the dead. First and most notable is the one to John Bunyan (died 1688), the author of *Pilgrim's Progress*. This was erected in 1851 and was, according to the inscription in its west panel, 'restored by public subscription under the presidency of the Right Honourable the

Earl of Shaftesbury May 1862'. There is however some doubt whether Bunyan was originally buried in this spot as it is recorded that he was interred in the vault owned by his friend John Strudwick in whose house he died. John Strudwick's daughter married the Rev Robert Bragge, who became Minister of the City Temple Congregational Church in 1697 and who died in 1737. The Bragge family tomb was on the spot where the Bunyan Memorial now stands. As a number of members of the family were buried there, it seems reasonable to assume that when the Strudwick vault was closed Bunyan's body was transferred to this grave.

Another striking memorial is the red granite obelisk which was erected to the memory of the Rev Joseph Hart (died 1765) in 1875 and bears the inscription 'Erected by lovers of Hart's hymns published in 1759 and still highly prized by the Church of God. The author's remains are interred in this spot as the original stone yet remains to show. Joseph Hart Minister of the Gospel died 24th May 1765 aged 56.'

The third most famous monument is the Egyptian pillar of Sicilian marble which was erected in 1870 in memory of Daniel Defoe and which bears the following inscription:

'DANIEL DE FOE: born 1661, died 1731, author of *Robinson Crusoe*. This monument is the result of an appeal, in the *Christian World* newspaper, to the boys and girls of England for funds to place a suitable memorial upon the grave of Daniel De Foe. It represents the united contributions of seventeen hundred persons. September 1870.'

Another tomb which one cannot fail to notice is that of Dame Mary Page (died 1728) which bears the following panels:

South Panel 'Here lyes Dame Mary Page,
Relict of Sir Gregory Page, Bart.
She departed this life March 11, 1728,
In the 56 year of her age.'

North Panel 'In 67 months she was tapped 66 times,
Had taken away 240 gallons of water,
Without ever repining at her case,
Or ever fearing the operation.'

From a host of other names there stand out those of Praise-God Bare-bones (died 1680) who gave his name to the Barebones Parliament of 1653; Dr Thomas Goodwin (died 1680) who is generally regarded as the founder of the City Temple Congregational Church, and his friend Dr John (Thankful) Owen (died 1683) who was buried in the same grave; Dr Daniel Williams (died 1716) the great Librarian; Mrs Susanna Wesley (died 1742), the mother of John and Charles Wesley and of seventeen other children; Isaac Watts D.D. (died 1748), the author of 'O God, our help in ages past'; Lady Anne Erskine (died 1804), daughter of the Earl of Buchan and friend and companion of the Countess of Huntingdon and trustee of her chapels after her death; and the great poet and painter William Blake (died 1827) and his wife (died 1831). In addition many members of the family of Oliver Cromwell are buried here, a family vault being erected by his grandson Henry.

Finally there is the tomb of the Rev John Rippon D.D. (died 1836 aged eighty-six years) who was for sixty-three years Pastor of the Baptist Church in Carter Lane, Southwark and who also merits remembrance for his activity in preserving the inscriptions on the tombs, as a result of which a record of these is still extant in the College of Heralds. This activity has been graphically described in the following extract from an eighteenth-century diary:

'We went into the ground by the old Royal (now City) Road – not our usual way. There we found a worthy man known to Mr Wilks, Mr Rippon by name, who was laid down upon his side between two graves, and writing out the epitaphs word for word. He had an ink-horn in his button-hole, and a pen and a book. He tells us that he has taken most of the old inscriptions, and that he will, if God be pleased to spare his days, do all, notwithstanding it is a grievous labour, and the writing is hard to make out by reason of the oldness of the cutting in some, and defacings of other stones. It is a labour of love to him, and when he is gathered to his fathers, I hope some one will go on with the work.'

It is satisfactory to know that he lived to complete his self-imposed task and that the result of his labours has not been lost. Of these the two following examples have been chosen. The first has about it echoes of the tribulations of St Paul and the second is a fine example of eighteenth-century moralizing.

'Here lyeth the body of FRANCIS SMITH, Bookseller, who in his Youth was settled in a separate Congregation, where he sustained, between the Years of 1659 and 1688, great persecution by Imprisonment, Exile, and large Fines laid on Ministers and Meeting Houses, and for printing and promoting Petitions for calling of a Parliament, with several Things against Popery, and after nearly 40 Imprisonments, he was fined £500 for printing and selling the Speech of a Noble Peer, and Three Times Corporeal Punishment. For the said fine he was 5 years in the King's Bench; His hard Duress there, utterly impaired his Health. He dyed Housekeeper in the Custom-House December the 22nd, 1691.'

The second reads quite simply:

'JOHANNES ANTRUM.
Obiit 15 Jan 1704.
Behold thy self by me,
Such one was I, as thou;
And thou in Time shalt be
Even Dust, as I am now.
Aetatis suae 54.'

C

🎕 CHARTERHOUSE,
CHARTERHOUSE SQUARE EC1

Charterhouse and Charterhouse Square stand on the thirteen acres of land outside the City walls which Sir Walter de Manny bought in 1349 to provide a burial-ground for victims of the plague, known as the Black Death, which ravaged England in the fourteenth century. He also added a chapel which in 1371 became a Carthusian foundation. Stow, whose statistics are notably erratic, says that over 100,000 people were buried here and that he himself had seen an inscription on the stone cross standing in the burial-ground to the effect that over 50,000 were buried in 1349 alone.

The monastery was dissolved in 1537 and in 1611 Thomas Sutton, Queen Elizabeth's Master of Ordnance, bought the property and endowed it as a school and a home for eighty men pensioners. In 1872 the school moved to Godalming but the pensioners' home remains. It is still private property and is one of the most beautiful undisturbed treasures left in the City. It can only be visited on limited occasions.

At its northern end, bounding the Clerkenwell Road, is the burial place of the pensioners. It is no longer in use but forms a quiet little garden with tombstones, no longer legible, along the wall.

🎕 CHELSEA OLD CHURCH,
CHEYNE WALK SW3

The church of All Saints, Chelsea, sometime known as St Luke's, but today invariably called Chelsea Old Church, possesses the smallest churchyard garden outside the City and one of the most attractive. There are only three seats and very little grass but in the summer it is full of flowers, tended by a team of church volunteers.

It is not known when the first church was built, but in 1670, when Wren was so busy rebuilding the City churches, it was substantially enlarged to meet the needs of a growing neighbourhood; the west end of the nave and the tower were pulled down and the church extended westwards. It was then that it became known for a time as St Luke's. The church was almost completely demolished by land mines in an air raid in 1941. After the war it was rebuilt on the plans of the original building.

Before the building of the Embankment in 1874 there had been no great distance between the church and the river and the churchyard was a larger and more public place. A footpath came up from the river, leading by steps past the Sloane Memorial and along the south wall of the church. Between the church and the river there now stands the recently erected monument to Sir Thomas More. Inside the garden at the south-east corner is the handsome memorial to another of Chelsea's best-known citizens, Sir Hans Sloane (died 1753), the famous physician and collector, who founded the British Museum. The Memorial, an urn entwined with serpents, bears the following inscription:

'To the memory of Sir Hans Sloane Bart. President of the Royal Society and of the College of Physicians, who in the year of our Lord 1753, the 92nd year of his age without the least pain of body and with a conscious serenity of mind, ended a virtuous and beneficent life. This monument was erected by his two daughters Eliza Cadogan and Sarah Stanley.'

Nearby is the memorial to Philip Miller, 'sometime Curator of the Botanical Garden Chelsea and Author of the Gardeners Dictionary; died December 18 1771 aged 70 and buried on the north side of the churchyard'. This memorial was erected by Fellows of the Linnaean and Horticultural Societies of London in 1815.

Along the south wall of the church is a series of monuments to the family of Edward Chamberlayne LL.D. (died 1703) who had nine children and wrote six books. He ordered some of his books to be covered with wax and buried with him in the hope that they might 'be of use in time to come'. Unfortunately no trace of the books could be found a hundred years later. His son John was responsible for publishing 'The Lord's Prayer in 100 languages'. His only daughter Anne Spragge (died 1692) fought, according to her tablet, under her brother Peregrine Clifford Chamberlayne against the French for six hours in a fire ship on 30 June 1690.

Sir John Fielding (died 1780), the famous blind magistrate who introduced the Bow Street runners, was also buried here.

🦁 CHELSEA BURIAL-GROUND, KING'S ROAD SW3

In 1719, after George I had closed the King's Road, its use was preserved by a successful petition to the Lords of the Treasury by Sir Hans Sloane, although it did not become a public road until 1830. Fourteen years later in 1733 he presented to the parish an area of land on the north side of the road between Sydney Street and Dovehouse Street to provide a burial-ground and a site for the workhouse. (It appears to have been a natural step for the rational philanthropists of the eighteenth century to place one beside the other. The same thing occurred in the parishes of both St Marylebone and St George, Hanover Square.)

The burial-ground was enlarged in 1790 by Charles, 3rd Baron and 1st Earl of Cadogan, the son of Elizabeth Sloane, daughter and co-heir of Sir Hans Sloane, from whom he inherited the Manor of Chelsea.

It ceased to be a burial-ground in 1824 when the new churchyard of St Luke's church came into use. It subsequently became the garden of the workhouse before being converted into the little public garden which it is today.

On the edge of the burial-ground there formerly stood a pump which, somewhat incongruously, was famous for its clear sparkling water.

In 1977 the garden was redesigned to provide a more open space and named Dovehouse Green.

CHRISTCHURCH, BROADWAY, WESTMINSTER SW1

There is little to suggest to the passenger riding along Victoria Street on the top of an omnibus that the small garden at the corner of Broadway was a burial-ground for centuries. There is now no church nor are there any gravestones to be seen in the garden, although a discerning eye will find some lined up in an enclosed space outside the northern boundary.

In fact a chapel dedicated to St Mary Magdalene stood somewhere in this area, then known as Tuthill Fields, as long ago as the thirteenth century. At the time of the dissolution of the monasteries Henry VIII placed this chapel and the monastic lands in Tuthill Fields under the control of the Dean and Chapter of Westminster Abbey. Stow in 1598 described this chapel as 'now wholly ruinated'. In 1631 the building of a new chapel was begun at the northern end of Tuthill Fields. This was completed in 1636 with the support of Archbishop Laud. It seems likely that this new chapel was built on or near the site of the original chapel, although no evidence of this has been forthcoming. The new chapel is shown on William Faithorne's Map of Westminster, published in 1658, under the description of 'New church in Tuttle Fields', but it was more generally known as the New Chapel. It is said that it remained unconsecrated until after the Restoration of Charles II and that during the Commonwealth it was used as a stable. It is not easy however to reconcile this with the entry in Pepys's Diary of 18 July 1665 in which he writes:

> 'I was much troubled this day to hear at Westminster how the officers do bury the dead in the open Tuttlefields, pretending want of room elsewhere; whereas the New-Chapel church-yard was walled in at the public charge in the last plague-time merely for want of room, and now none but such as are able to pay dear for it can be buried there.'

The 'last plague-time' had been in 1647.

In regard to burial in the churchyard for those able 'to pay dear for it', a separate place of burial for plague victims cut off from the rest of the churchyard was provided, protected by a wall, deep ditch and bridge.

It seems clear that the original churchyard was considerably larger than it remains today. An area 'in the open Tuttlefields' to which Pepys refers became one of the plague pits. This remains an open space to this day, now forming part of the playing fields of Westminster School.

One of the more interesting people to be buried here was Ignatius Sancho (died 1780) who is thus described in the very entertaining *Nollekens and his Times* by J. T. Smith, published in 1828:

> 'In June 1780, Mr Nollekens took me to the house of Ignatius Sancho, who kept a grocer's, or rather chandler's, shop at No. 20 Charles Street, Westminster: a house still standing at the south-west corner of Crown Court. This extraordinary literary character, a Negro, was born on board a slave-ship in 1729. He was patronised by the Duke of Montague, who made him his butler, and left him a legacy and an annuity at his death, when he took the shop above mentioned. In his leisure hours he indulged his taste for music, painting and literature; which procured him the acquaintance of several persons of distinction. He was the author of some pieces of poetry, and a tract on the Theory of Music; and his letters, with his life, by Jekyll, were published after his death, for the benefit of his family.'

Here too were buried Sir William Waller (died 1668), the Parliamentary General; Colonel Thomas Blood (died 1680), the adventurer who attempted to steal the Crown jewels; and Margaret Batten (died 1739), who was reputed to be 136 years old at the time of her death.

In the churchyard there is an interesting monument to the Suffragette movement. It is a curious piece of modern sculpture which bears the following inscription:

> 'This Tribute was erected by the Suffragette Fellowship to commemorate the courage and perseverance of all those men and women who in the long struggle for votes for women selflessly braved derision opposition and ostracism many enduring physical violence and suffering.'

Nearby Caxton Hall was historically associated with female suffrage meetings and deputations to Parliament.

The New Chapel again fell into disrepair in the nineteenth century and in 1841 the Dean and Chapter disclaimed any further responsibility for it; in 1843 it was demolished. A larger church, to be known as Christchurch, was built in its place but this in turn was pulled down in 1954.

❦ CHRISTCHURCH, NEWGATE STREET EC1

The ruins of Christchurch stand on land originally given to the Franciscan Grey Friars by certain devout citizens at the beginning of the thirteenth century. The first church was built about 1225 and a new church a hundred years later under the patronage of Queen Margaret, the second wife of Edward I. On the dissolution of the monasteries by Henry VIII the King allowed the whole property to pass to 'the mayor and commonalty of London' including '... the hospital of St Bartholomew in West Smithfield, the church of the same, the lead, bells and ornaments of the same hospital, with all the messuages, tenements and appurtenances, the parishes of St Nicholas and St Ewin and so much of St Sepulchre's parish as is within Newgate' and the same 'were made one parish church in the Gray Friars church, and called Christ's Church, founded by Henry VIII'. So their church became a parish church and their home, in 1552, under the patronage of Edward VI, a school – the original Christ's Hospital School, now in Sussex.

The church was destroyed by the Great Fire. It was rebuilt in 1687 by Wren but as a much smaller church limited to the site of the old choir, the area of the nave being incorporated into the churchyard. Greyfriars Passage, which gives access to the garden from Newgate Street, marks the division between the old choir and nave. Wren's church was almost totally destroyed in what was the worst night attack on the City on 29 December 1940; only the tower and spire survived. The church is not to be rebuilt and a garden has been made in the ruins. It is now proposed to adapt the tower for use as offices.

The main garden lies to the west of the ruins where the old churchyard was. Here there is a good walk, flanked by mature trees and paved with tombstones, along what is probably the centre aisle of the old nave. There are seats along the edge of Newgate Street.

Because the old Grey Friars church was under royal patronage and because it was thought that entrance to Heaven might be more easily achieved through the Friary portals, this was a favourite place of burial before the dissolution of the monasteries. Four queens were buried here – Queen Margaret, who founded the second church (died 1318); Queen Isabella, wife of Edward II (died 1358); and her daughter Joanna, Queen of Scotland (died 1362); and Isabella, Queen of Man; also Princess Beatrix, daughter of Henry III (died 1260); Princess Isabel, daughter of Edward III (died c. 1379); Sir John Philpot, grocer, mayor 1378, who 'sent ships to the sea, and scoured it of pirates, taking many of them prisoner' (died 1384); John, Duke of Bourbon and Anjou, Earl of Claremond, Montpensier, and Baron Beaujeu, 'who was taken prisoner at Agincourt, kept prisoner eighteen years and deceased 1433'; and Sir Thomas Malory, Knight, compiler of *Le Morte d'Arthur* (died c. 1470). Later came Elizabeth Barton, the 'Holy Maid of Kent', executed at Tyburn 1534: Laurence Sheriff, founder of Rugby School (died 1567); and the Rev James Boyer, Charles Lamb's Headmaster at Christ's Hospital (died 1814).

ST CLEMENT DANES, STRAND WC2

The origins of the church are not known, but its foundation probably ranks next to St Pancras in order of seniority. Stow has a story that in the reign of King Ethelred (978–1016) a marauding group of Danes, who had destroyed the abbey of Chertsey in Surrey, were all killed 'in a place which is called the church of the Danes'. It seems to be established that by the time King Hardicanute came to the throne in 1039 there was a stone-built church standing here.

The story of the churchyard may be said to start with an incident which occurred soon after this. Hardicanute caused the body of his half-brother Harold I, whom he had succeeded, to be taken out of Westminster Abbey and thrown into the Thames. His body was recovered by a fisherman and buried in this churchyard.

Ogilby and Morgan's Map of London, published in 1676, shows St Clement Danes with a large churchyard on its north, east and west sides. It is probable that the statue of W. E. Gladstone, which faces west at the eastern junction of Aldwych and the Strand, stands in what was once a

The Suffragette Monument – Christchurch, Westminster.

This tribute
is erected by the
Suffragette
Fellowship to
commemorate
the courage and
perseverance of
all those men and
women who in the
long struggle for
votes for women
selflessly braved
derision, opposition
and ostracism, many
enduring physical
violence and suffering

Nearby Caxton Hall was
historically associated
with women's advance
to citizenship

St Giles, Cripplegate, from the South West, c.1835.

St Giles, Cripplegate, at the time of the Great Plague in which this parish suffered more than any other with 4838 deaths.

part of the churchyard. Today the small area of grass interspersed with a few trees which surrounds the church hardly qualifies for the description of a garden. There is however a stone seat against the east end of the church looking up Fleet Street and at the back of the statue of Dr Johnson which stands in the centre of the green wedge of grass.

The old church was outside the boundaries of the Great Fire, but it was rebuilt in 1680 to plans prepared by Wren. It was totally destroyed by a number of air attacks in the 1939–45 War. Rebuilt in 1955 it was reconsecrated as the church of the Royal Air Force.

Anne Donne, the wife of John Donne (died 1617), was buried here and he preached the funeral oration. Two dramatists, Thomas Otway (died 1685) and Nathaniel Lee (died 1692); three actors, John Lowen (died 1653), William Mountford (murdered 1692) and James Spiller (died 1730); Nicholas Byer, a painter and a Dane (died 1681); Edward Pierce, a sculptor (died 1698); and George Sale, translator of the Koran (died 1736), were all also buried here. Dr Johnson, who was buried in Westminster Abbey, worshipped here for many years – hence the statue in the garden.

ST CLEMENT, EASTCHEAP EC3

The garden of this church, dedicated to the patron saint of seamen (who was martyred by being thrown into the sea attached to an anchor), is a tiny fragment of the old churchyard at the east end of the church. It is approached by a small passage from Clements Lane and is entirely surrounded by office buildings. It comprises a single tree, which offers some shade in summer, and a few rose bushes; and it is a quiet retreat. Two tombstones remain – one being that of John Poynder, who died 11 April 1800, aged forty-eight, and of his four children who all died in infancy.

18th century burial-ground of St George, Bloomsbury and St George the Martyr, Queen Square.

ST DUNSTAN-IN-THE-EAST,
ST DUNSTAN'S HILL EC3

This is one of the more adventurous essays by the City Corporation in garden-making, the ruins of the old church destroyed in the 1939–45 War having been successfully incorporated into a garden created from the old churchyard and the church site.

The original church, probably of the thirteenth century, was described by Stow as 'a fair and large church of an ancient building, and within a large churchyard; it hath a great parish of many rich merchants, and other occupiers of divers trades namely salters and ironmongers'.

This church was destroyed in the Great Fire but the walls, having been thoroughly repaired with Portland stone earlier in the seventeenth century, survived, so that only the tower and spire had to be rebuilt. This gave rise to an interesting and charming piece of Wren work in the Gothic style built to harmonize with the fourteenth-century architecture. In the 1939–45 War it was the turn of the tower and spire to survive and these make a fine background for the garden.

A number of paths have been laid and there is a low fountain in the centre of the former nave. The garden is well planted and there are plenty of seats. It is a good sunny spot, being more or less open on the south side, and there is an excellent view of the Monument to the west.

Here were buried Sir Bartholomew James, draper, mayor 1479, who in 1470 was knighted on the field by Edward IV along with eleven other aldermen and Thomas Urswike the Recorder for their conduct when Thomas the Bastard Fauconbridge with a riotous company set upon the City at Aldgate, Bishopsgate and elsewhere; and Admiral Sir John Lawson, who died of wounds received in the Battle of Lowestoft against the Dutch in 1665.

Only one tombstone which can now be identified remains. This is the stone, ornamented with a fine coat of arms, of Captain Nicholas Batcheler who died 31 December 1722, aged sixty. The stone also commemorates his wife Mary (died 1723), three of his children and one grandchild. At the foot of the stone has been added, in what appears to be the hand of another and less skilled stonemason, 'Here lyeth also the Body of Anne Blackall, a Beloved Relation'.

ST DUNSTAN-IN-THE-WEST, FLEET STREET EC4

All that remains of the churchyard of St Dunstan-in-the-West is a small untidy yard fronting on to Fleet Street. This however contains two satisfying pieces of sculpture – a bust of Lord Northcliffe (1865–1922) and a statue of Queen Elizabeth I. The latter is the oldest outdoor statue in London north of the river. It formerly stood on Ludgate where it was placed in 1586 when the gate was rebuilt. The gate was pulled down in 1760 and the statue given to Sir Francis Gosling, alderman of the ward of Farringdon Without (in which the church stands), who in 1766 had it placed on the exterior of the church. There is also a tablet commemorating Izaac Walton who lived nearby in Fleet Street and was a vestryman and sidesman. His *The Compleat Angler* was published in the precincts of St Dunstan's churchyard in 1653.

St Dunstan's also had a burial-ground a little further north – in Bream Buildings. The site remains but is mainly enclosed and in private occupation. There are some good trees along the roadside and a number of tombstones remain. The opportunity of creating another small garden appears to have been lost.

ST ETHELBURGA THE VIRGIN, BISHOPSGATE EC2

This, the smallest City church remaining, hides one of the secret gardens of the City, which can only be reached through the church and vestry. It is a real haven of quiet, being enclosed on all sides. There is a cloister along the north wall and in the centre a fountain – the gift of the Billiter Literary Society in memory of the Rev W. F. Geikie Cobb – Rector from 1900 to 1941. There are also some commemorative seats.

There has been a church here since the thirteenth century but the present church, which was one of the few to escape the Great Fire, is of the fifteenth century.

ST GEORGE, BLOOMSBURY, BLOOMSBURY WAY WC1 AND ST GEORGE THE MARTYR, QUEEN SQUARE WC1

Both these two churches were consecrated as part of Queen Anne's proposals to provide fifty new churches – to be paid for by a tax on coal. Neither has any churchyard but they shared a common burial-ground – the northern half being allocated to St George, Bloomsbury and the other to St George the Martyr. This ground is on the north of the Foundling Hospital site and is approached from Gray's Inn Road by Heathcote Street and by Handel Street on the west. When it was acquired in 1713 it formed part of a country meadow. It was from this burial-ground that the first indicted case of body-snatching occurred in 1777. Today it is a pleasant garden and there is no longer a line of demarcation between the two churches.

After its closure as a place of burial the ground fell into decay. In 1872, Mr F. T. Cansick, who is responsible for preserving the wording of many of the memorials in this garden, wrote: 'The cemetery of St George the Martyr ... is in a very bad state – the stones falling over and broken, the trees uncut and the wood grown wild. It has all the appearance of a wilderness, and is a standing disgrace to the parish. The cemetery of the wealthy parish of St George's Bloomsbury also joins the above, and is a little better cared for but in many instances the inscriptions are almost obliterated.' This note of censure did not fall on deaf ears, although the effect was not immediate. In 1885 the burial-ground was leased by the then Rector of St George, Bloomsbury, the Rev Fieldflower Goe, who later became Bishop of Melbourne, Australia, to the local authority for 999 years at an annual rent of one shilling, which continues to be paid. He would doubtless approve of the position today and be pleased to see the gardens well laid out with flowering shrubs and flowerbeds.

As Mr Cansick recorded, there were a number of impressive family vaults here, adorned with their coats of arms. Many of the vaults have been left undisturbed and some of the coats of arms are still to be seen, but almost all of the inscriptions are illegible. The most famous name is that of Anne Cromwell (died 1727), granddaughter of Oliver Cromwell, being the daughter of his son Richard. Her tomb has been accorded the dignity of a new stone. Near to it there is an impressive obelisk but the inscription on it can no longer be read. Other names include the author, John Campbell (died 1755); the painter, Jonathan Richardson the Younger (died 1771); Peter Donaldson (died 1812), 'first Master Cook to His Majesty [George III] and upwards of 40 years in his service'; and Zachary Macaulay (died 1838), father of the historian and a philanthropist who worked for the abolition of the slave trade.

Of the inscriptions preserved by Mr Cansick, that of the Brand family is an interesting epitome of the life of a middle-class family of the time. It read:

'Sacred to the Memory of Lieut. George Rowley Brand, R.N., Commander of His Majesty's schooner, *Unique*, Who, after receiving upward of 30 wounds, In various actions, was killed on the 23rd of February, 1806, at the early age of 24, Whilst gallantly leading his men to board a French vessel of double his force. The French in admiration of his bravery, Buried him with military honours, at Guadaloupe.

Also of Robert Frederick Brand, who died 20th of May 1808 aged 9 years.

Also of Lieut. Thomas Dickinson Brand, R.N., who, after a long and painful illness, caused by the climate of India, died on the 12th of November 1830, aged 36 years.

Also of Alexander Brand, Father of the above, who died the 7th of April 1859,★ aged 83 years.

Also of Ann, Relict of the above named Alexander Brand, who died on the 15th December 1847, aged 91 years.'

★ 1859 clearly a misreading for 1839.

THE BURIAL-GROUND OF ST GEORGE, HANOVER SQUARE W1

Turning down South Audley Street from Mount Street one comes immediately to the Grosvenor Chapel. This is one of the rare surviving examples of the proprietary chapels of the eighteenth century. It was built in 1730 as part of the Grosvenor Square development begun in 1721, and, as Sir John Summerson has remarked, 'it resembles more than any other surviving London church the kind of thing which emigrant builders were putting up across the sea in New England'. It is certainly a charming sight with its toy-brick western façade, particularly when viewed from Hyde Park along Aldford Street.

It would be natural to assume that the garden which lies behind it originally comprised its churchyard, but this is not the case. These gardens, as their name implies, were formerly the burial-ground of St George, Hanover Square. This was another of the Queen Anne churches, built between 1712 and 1714 – just before the Grosvenor Square development began. As Hanover Square was already a built-up area it was natural that a burial-ground should be sought in the open fields which lay to the west and this site was acquired from Sir Richard Grosvenor in 1725 for £300.

Walking through the garden one can still see a few gravestones but there are a great many more not immediately visible. The garden stands a little above the basement rooms of some of the adjacent buildings and the old gravestones have been used to line the sloping edges of the lawns, noticeably along the northern and south-eastern sides. In place of the old stones there is another kind of memorial today in the wooden seats which are numerous in this garden. Most of these have been given in memory of those, many of them American, who in their lifetime found pleasure in these gardens, but some also in gratitude from people who still live to enjoy them. These seats beneath the fine trees, which provide ample shade in summertime, are much patronized by both workers and residents in the district. The gardens are exceptionally well placed, being approached from four different entrances – one in South Audley Street, north of the Grosvenor Chapel, two from Mount Street and the fourth from Farm Street on the south past the St George's Church of England school.

63

When this burial-ground became full, which happened in 1763, another large ground of some four acres was bought in the country beyond Tyburn on the Uxbridge Road (now the Bayswater Road). This was consecrated in 1764.

Writing in 1892, George Clinch, in his *History of Mayfair and Belgravia*, said 'The burial-ground of St George's, Hanover Square is situated just off Oxford Street, near the Marble Arch, and between Albion Street and Stanhope Street. It is a beautifully quiet and secluded area, almost entirely enclosed by tall houses, well wooded with a profusion of trees and ornamented with some borders of old-fashioned flowers.' At the time he wrote, the old eighteenth-century mortuary chapel still remained.

From about 1923 until 1939 the churchyard was used as the archery ground of the Royal Toxophilite Society.

In the property development activity which followed the 1939–45 War the Church Commissioners are reputed to have received an offer of £1,000,000 for the site. Be that as it may, the site was sold and re-developed and most of the ground is now covered by a block of flats known as St George's Fields. There remains a small area of the burial-ground on the north side which can be reached from Albion Street. This forms a garden with a number of tombstones leaning against the north and east walls. It is however a private garden, at present used by the Hyde Park Nursery School. Permission to enter can be obtained.

The tombstone of the most famous person buried here does not appear to have been preserved. Laurence Sterne (died 18 March 1768) was buried on 22 March, and according to popular belief his body was snatched by body-snatchers on 24 March. Traill in his *Life of Sterne* says that the body was sold to a Professor of Anatomy at Cambridge, who invited some friends to witness a demonstration he would perform, not knowing that one of his friends had also been a friend of Sterne and was to recognize the corpse. In more recent years this gruesome story has been discredited. At a later date a somewhat inaccurate memorial stone bearing the following inscription was erected:

'Alas Poor Yorick. Near to this place lies the body of the Revd Laurence Sterne dyed Sept. 13. 1768 aged 53 years. This monument stone was erected to the memory of the deceased by two

Brother Masons, for although he did not live to be a member of their Society, yet all his incomparable Performances evidently proved him to have acted by Rule and Square; they rejoice in the opportunity of perpetuating his high and unapproachable character to after ages.

W. and S.'

ᛘ   ST GILES, CRIPPLEGATE EC2

In 1875 Thomas Hardy wrote of the churchyard of St Giles with its 'untainted leaves of the lime and plane trees and the newly sprung grass [which] had in the sun a brilliancy of beauty that was brought into extraordinary prominence by the sable earth showing here and there ...' Today after one hundred years and two world wars, the scene is very different – no grass, no flowerbeds, no sable earth and only a few trees. The whole area of the churchyard has been paved and only one tomb remains – to the south of the church. Nevertheless nothing can alter the magnificence of the site on which the church stands – in a noble piazza with the re-developed Barbican as a backcloth and a stretch of the old City wall to the south. Here may be seen the remains of a bastion where the wall turned from north to east. Here too between the church and the wall a stretch of water shows where the 'town ditch' traced its course outside the wall. Stow also refers to a spring of clear water 'near unto the parsonage on the west side'. It has been suggested that the fact that water was virtually drawn out of the churchyard was the reason why this parish suffered more severely from the Great Plague of 1665 than any other in the City. The number of deaths registered in that year totalled 8069 (of which 4838 were attributed to the plague) and the level of the churchyard was raised two feet. It should be remembered that in Stow's time this was a large and fashionable parish having, as he says, 'more than 1800 householders and above 8000 communicants'.

The fourteenth-century church was badly damaged by fire in 1545 but escaped the Great Fire of 1666, only to be almost totally destroyed in the air attacks of 1940. It has since been rebuilt.

The tomb which remains is that of Sir William Staines, Lord Mayor

1801, died 1807, who, as his memorial inside the church records, rose from humble beginnings to hold the highest office in the City. Before the 1939–45 War a statue of John Milton (died 1674), who was buried here, stood on a tall plinth outside the church. It was damaged in the air raids and has since been repaired but unfortunately not restored to its former place.

Milton was not the only famous person to be buried here. There were John Foxe, author of the famous *Book of Martyrs* (died 1587); Sir Martin Frobisher, the Elizabethan Admiral and hero of the defeat of the Spanish Armada, who died of wounds sustained in action off Brest in 1594; and John Speed (died 1629), the best known of the early cartographers. Worthy of mention too is Edmund Harrison (died 1666 aged seventy-seven), Embroiderer to three kings – James I, Charles I and Charles II, who: 'having lived above 40 years a bachelor had to wife Jane the eldest daughter of Thomas Godfrey late of Hodeford in the county of Kent Esquire by whom he had issue 12 sons and 9 daughters of whom at the time of his death were living 3 sons Godfrey, Edmund and Peter and two daughters Sarah and Jane'.

ST GILES-IN-THE-FIELDS, HOLBORN WC2

The churches of St Giles-in-the Fields and St Martin-in-the-Fields, when first built, stood in the fields between the City and the neighbouring medieval villages, and were so named.

Early in the twelfth century Queen Matilda, the wife of Henry I, founded a hospital for lepers in an isolated spot outside the City, which now comprises the triangle formed between Charing Cross Road, Shaftesbury Avenue and St Giles's High Street. The chapel of this hospital was to become, on the dissolution of the monasteries by Henry VIII, the parish church of St Giles-in-the-Fields. Since then the church has been twice rebuilt. The present charming Georgian building was erected in 1734.

The churchyard, which was enlarged in 1628, lies mainly on the south side of the church. It now forms a pleasant garden with rosebeds, an herbaceous border and plenty of seats. There is also a separate playground for children in its south-west corner. Access is from both the High Street and New Compton Street.

There are a number of tombstones which are not legible. One, however, has been restored and, whilst the inscription is in doggerel verse, it merited restoration as recording the contemporary tribute to Richard Pendrell, who played a leading part in the escape of Charles II after the Battle of Worcester in 1651. He died on 8 February 1671. The restored stone reads:

'Hold Passenger, Here's Shrouded in this Herse
Unparalled Pendrell Thro the Universe.
Like when the Eastern Star from Heaven gave Light
To Three Lost Kings, so he in such dark Night
To Britain's Monarch lost by Adverse War
On Earth Appeared a Second Eastern Star.
A Pole. A Stem. In her Rebellious Main,
A Pilot to her Royal Sovereign Came.
Now to Triumph in Heaven's Eternal Sphere
He is advanced for his Just Steerage here.
Whilst Albion's Chronicles with Matchless Fame
Embalm the Story of Great Pendrell's Name.'

Here too were buried the twelve Catholic martyrs, victims of the Titus Oates Plot of 1678–81 – Oliver Plunket, Archbishop of Armagh, seven priests and four laymen, all of whom, except one who died in arrest, were executed at Tyburn.

Other names include George Chapman, the Elizabethan dramatist and the translator of Homer and inspirer of Keats's sonnet 'On first looking into Chapman's Homer':

'Yet never did I breathe its pure serene
Till I heard Chapman speak out loud and bold.'

What an epitaph. He died in 1634, followed by four other seventeenth-century poets or dramatists – Lord Herbert (died 1648); James Shirley (died 1666 as a result of fleeing from the Great Fire); Andrew Marvell (died 1678); and Sir Charles Sedley (died 1701). Amongst eighteenth-century names were Edward Dennis, virtually the last Tyburn hangman, who died in 1786 three years after executing William Ryland, the engraver, for forgery (the last execution at Tyburn, not by Dennis, took place on 7 November 1783); and Luke Hansard, the printer of the House of Commons Reports from 1774 to 1803 – in his own way the most famous of all Parliamentary names. He died in 1828 and so may have been buried in the parish burial-ground adjoining St Pancras church.

These are only a few of many names, and this is one of those churchyard gardens where one could well sit and consider the innumerable unnamed who have been buried in it. First would be the lepers who had died in the old hospital, then those executed at Tyburn who, after 1650, were buried here. (Before that date it had been the practice for the condemned to stop at the gate of the hospital on their way from Newgate to Tyburn to take their last drink of ale from the 'St Giles' Bowl' offered there by way of comfort and temporary respite.) Then there would have been the victims of the Great Plague, which started in this parish in November 1664. It was thought to have been brought over from Holland in goods which were unpacked at a house in what was then known as Ashlin's Place, an alley off the west side of the upper end of Drury Lane (almost opposite Stukeley Street). In 1665 3216 deaths from the plague were recorded in this parish and of these 1361 were buried in this churchyard in the month of July. (It is good to know that the Rector Dr Boreman and the parish doctor Dr Boghurst, like Samuel Pepys, stayed at their posts, and, like Pepys, survived.)

Later came the deaths of a number of French Huguenots who, after 1685, following the Edict of Nantes, sought refuge in England and settled in the new houses being erected by Dr Nicholas Barbon, son of Praise-God Barebones. He was not only a physician and Member of Parliament but also the first speculative builder. These houses were put up in St Giles's Fields on the other side of what is now Charing Cross Road but was then a lane known as Hog Lane.

It was this active building which took place over the following fifty years and, in particular, the development of Georgian London in the handsome squares further west, which led to the gradual decline of this area of seventeenth-century fashion into the slum of the eighteenth century so vividly portrayed in Hogarth's 'Gin Lane', painted in 1751, with the neighbouring church of St George, Bloomsbury in the background.

The area lying immediately to the north of the church became known as 'St Giles' Rookery' and for nearly a hundred years was regarded as one of the worst slums of London, the home of beggars, rogues and prostitutes, many living in cellars, whose only consolation in life was the consumption of gin, which at this time was being produced in vast quantities and sold almost everywhere for next to nothing – 'Drunk for a penny, dead drunk for tuppence.' The year 1751 probably marked the turning point, but it was not until the construction of New Oxford Street in 1847 that the trouble was effectively ended. The Burial Registers for the years 1815 to 1826 contain 8000 names, many of them being infants; at this time the population of St Giles's was some 30,000.

ST HELEN, BISHOPSGATE EC3

St Helen was described by its vicar, the Rev J. E. Cox in 1876 as having been the most aristocratic parish of Old London with St Olave, Hart Street ranking next. More recently it has been described as 'the Westminster Abbey of the City' by reason of the magnificence of its tombs. What remains of its churchyard is a modest affair like a neat suburban front garden before its west doors, but it is a very pleasant place to sit away from the bustle of Bishopsgate. There are sunny seats in front of the church and shady green grass to look upon. A few tombstones remain as a reminder of mortality. There is one to 'Joseph Lem citizen of London Departed this life 21 August 1686'; and another to 'George Low upward of 60 years an inhabitant of this parish Departed this life 13 June 1783 aged 69'; and the most recent one to 'Mary Freeman died 4 August 1831'.

The church is one of the earliest and finest of the City churches, escaping both the Great Fire and the 1939–45 air attacks, and has not suffered rebuilding. According to tradition a pagan temple stood here originally and the Emperor Constantine, on his conversion to Christianity, caused a church to be built on the site and dedicated to his mother Helena, the reputed discoverer of the Holy Cross.

To select from the many famous buried here is invidious but it is hard to omit Adam Frances, mercer, mayor 1352 and 1353, who, as Stow records, 'procured an Act of Parliament that no known whore should wear any hood or attire on her head except red or striped cloth of divers colour'; Sir Thomas Gresham (died 1579), mercer, founder of the Royal Exchange; Sir Julius Caesar Adelmare (died 1636), Chancellor of the Exchequer and Master of the Rolls, whose tomb bears in Latin the astonishing inscription, which translated reads:

'Chancellor of the Exchequer and Master of the Rolls ... by this my act and deed confirm with my full consent that, by the Divine aid, I will willingly pay the debt of Nature as soon as it may please God. In Witness wherof I have fixed my hand and seal February 27th 1634. Jul. Caesar.

He paid this debt, being at the time of his death of the Privy Council of King Charles, also Master of the Rolls; truly pious, particularly learned, a refuge to the poor, abounding in love, most dear to his country, his children and his friends.

It is enrolled in Heaven.'

and Dame Abigail Laurence, the inscription on whose tomb reads:

'Dame Abigail Laurence late wife of Sir John Laurence Kt. and Alderman. She was the mother of 10 children; the nine first, being all daughters, she suckled at her own breasts. Her last a son died an infant. She died 16 June 1682.'

❧ HOLY TRINITY, BROMPTON SW3

Holy Trinity, consecrated in 1829, was the last London church to be provided with its own churchyard adjoining. At this time the church stood in comparatively open country and a large area was allocated as a churchyard. It was in use for only twenty-five years and there was no time for the usual encroachments to take place so that today there is a large garden on the north side of the church. This with its fine old trees, considerable area of grass and a few tombstones, retains something of the air of a village churchyard.

In 1896 the churchyard was described as 'having a neglected appearance'. It was reduced to the same state by the 1939–45 War and in the early 1950s it was decided to remove the gravestones to make a garden. Those buried here were re-interred in Brookwood Cemetery. Unlike most churchyard gardens this remains the property of the church and is maintained by parish volunteers.

ST JAMES, PICCADILLY W1

The principal entrance to the church and the only entrance to the churchyard garden is now from Piccadilly but the original entrance was from Jermyn Street. The church, which was consecrated in 1684, was built as part of the residential development carried out by Henry Jermyn 1st Earl of St Albans on land given to him by Charles II as a reward for his companionship in exile and support on his return. St James's Square was the focal point of the development and the church was built on the axis of the square with its entrance looking straight down York Street (now Duke of York Street). It was not until 1856 that this entrance was closed and a window substituted. The entrance gates remain.

There is now a good pair of wrought entrance gates in the north (Piccadilly) wall, erected at the time of the Coronation of King George VI. These lead into a paved courtyard which has been made of the northern part of the old churchyard. A few gravestones are incorporated in the paving and a number more have been placed along the north wall. There is an outdoor pulpit attached to the church. This was erected at the beginning of the present century but is not now in use. There is a good catalpa tree on the west side of the courtyard and a magnolia, some rose bushes and, sometimes in summer, some hops on the rectory side.

Another part of the churchyard (once known as the Green Churchyard) lies to the west of the church. It is considerably more elevated, due to the practice of adding extra soil to the surface when the churchyard was still in use. (It will be an odd turn of fate if this economy measure of an earlier century is now to provide an opportunity to construct shops beneath the churchyard as has been recently suggested.) The churchyard is now a Garden of Remembrance given 'To Commemorate the Fortitude of Londoners during the 1939–45 War'. This quiet spot with its green lawns, plenty of seats, a statue of Peace and an attractive fountain, is indeed an admirable memorial contrasting with the noise, the dirt and the distress of the air raids. The fountain, in the form of a dolphin, commemorates the donor of the garden – Viscount Southwood (died 1946), the newspaper proprietor and philanthropist, who started his career delivering newspapers and went on to found Odhams Press. His ashes and those of his widow are interred here.

Amongst those buried here in earlier times were Dr Thomas Sydenham (died 1689) who was known as the English Hippocrates and in whose honour the Sydenham Society was founded in the nineteenth century; the two Dutch marine painters William Van de Velde, father (died 1693) and son (died 1707); James Huysman, portrait painter (died 1696); Mrs Delaney, bluestocking and 'ingenious maker of paper flowers' (died 1768); James Christie, the auctioneer (died 1803); 'old Q', the Duke of Queensberry (died 1810); and James Gillray, the cartoonist (died 1815). (It is possible that one or more of the last three, having died after 1788, when the Hampstead Road burial-ground was opened, were buried there.)

ST JAMES'S GARDENS, HAMPSTEAD ROAD NW1

Like St Martin-in-the-Fields, St James, finding itself in the eighteenth century in a fully built up area, had to seek additional burial space further in the country. Under an Act of Parliament passed in 1788, the purchase of land adjoining the road to Hampstead was authorized. The Act also provided for the erection of a chapel together with a house as a residence for the officiating clergyman. The chapel was consecrated in 1793. The gardens formed from this burial-ground lie behind the Royal Temperance Hospital on the east side of the Hampstead Road close to the spot where the Tottenham Court Road Turnpike used to stand.

In 1864 the chapel was bought from St James by St Pancras for £2000 to provide one of the four new parish churches required under the re-organization of the old parish of St Pancras. In 1877 the burial-ground was opened as a public garden. In 1954 this parish was reunited with the parish of the new St Pancras church and the chapel closed.

There are few tombs to be seen. There is one of the Stebbings family, of whom the Rev Dr Henry Stebbings, a well-known historian of his time, was appointed Minister of the Chapel in 1836 and lived in the clergy-house until his death in 1883. Records of burial include the names of the painter George Morland (died 1804); Lt Col John Harris Cruger (died 1807) who, as his monument said, 'had been an inhabitant of the City of New York in North America and at the commencement of the Rebellion (disregarding all personal considerations) he took up arms in support of the Rights of this country'. It went on to record that he distinguished himself in the defence of the important Post of Ninety-six in South Carolina, in the action of the Eutwas and in the relief of the garrison of Fort Augusta; and General Sir John Floyd Bt (died 1818) 'whose military career in Germany and in India obtained the praises of his sovereign and the admiration of his brethren in arms'.

ST JOHN THE BAPTIST, WALBROOK EC4

Nothing of this churchyard remains except a memorial stone on the north side of Cloak Lane at the junction with Dowgate Hill. This reads:

'Sacred
to the memory of the dead
interred in the ancient church and churchyard
of St John the Baptist
upon Walbrook
during four centuries.
The formation of the District Railway
having necessitated the destruction of
the greater part of the churchyard.
All the human remains contained therein were carefully
collected and reinterred in a vault beneath this monument.
A.D. 1884.'

The church was built in the twelfth century. It was destroyed in the Great Fire and not rebuilt, but its site and churchyard continued in use as a place of burial until closed in the middle of the nineteenth century.

THE BURIAL-GROUND OF ST JOHN, CLERKENWELL, BENJAMIN STREET EC1

This is a charming and secluded garden tucked away to the north of Smithfield Market. It has an interesting history. The land was bequeathed by the Will of Simon Michel, who died in 1750, to the Priory church of St John, Clerkenwell to provide an additional burial-ground. It was consecrated in 1755 by the Bishop of Lincoln. The church of the Priory of the Knights Hospitaller of St John of Jerusalem was built shortly after the arrival of the Hospitallers in England in 1145. It was demolished, except the chancel and tower, in the reign of Edward VI after the dissolution of the Order in 1540. From that date the chancel was used for a variety of purposes, including the office of Master of the Revels – a kind of Elizabethan censor. At the start of the eighteenth century it was being used as a Presbyterian Meeting House until Simon Michel bought it in 1721. He repaired it, gave it a new roof and west front, and then sold it to Queen Anne's Church Commissioners to provide an additional parish church. In 1929 it ceased to be a parish church and reverted to the revived Order of St John of Jerusalem as the chapel of the Order. It was destroyed by a bomb in 1941 but has since been rebuilt.

The garden now contains all that can be asked of a garden. There are beautiful trees, flowering shrubs, fine flowerbeds, plenty of seats and a drinking fountain, and it is quiet and secluded. Only one tombstone remains, in the east wall, and it is indecipherable except for the date – 1815. There were until recently some more tombstones in the north wall, which has been demolished in connection with an adjoining redevelopment.

THE BURIAL-GROUND OF ST JOHN, SMITH SQUARE, HORSEFERRY ROAD SW1

The development of London moved to the south of Westminster Abbey in the early eighteenth century and another of the Queen Anne churches was allocated to this area. Here, in what was to become Smith Square, was built Thomas Archer's masterpiece, one of the rare baroque churches in London. It was completed in 1728 and dedicated to St John the Evangelist. The square, like the church, is exceptional. There is no central enclosed area with grass and trees; the church stands at the centre of the square and dominates it.

In Roque's 'Plan of the Cities of London and Westminster', published in 1746, the church is shown surrounded by a large open space described as the churchyard, but this was either very soon full or never intended as a place of burial, as soon after the church was completed the Vestry were looking elsewhere for a burial-ground. This was found for them by the Church Commissioners who acquired a site in Horseferry Road (then known as Market Street) which forms part of the present gardens. It was consecrated in 1731, just three years after the dedication of the church. All that remains of the original churchyard area in Smith Square is some flowerbeds in the angles of the cruciform church.

The burial-ground was soon found to be too small and the Vestry were looking for more land. This was thought to be too expensive and in consequence resort was had to the common practice of bringing in soil. In this case some details are available. An extra three feet of soil were added at a cost of £125. In 1758 a further overlaying was found necessary, but this time they were able to economize by using rubble from the rebuilding work which was going on at St Margaret, Westminster. The surface was again raised at the beginning of the nineteenth century, and in a further effort to reduce congestion the burial fees were put up fourfold. At last in 1823 some more land was bought from Lord Grosvenor for £2050 and the burial-ground enlarged to its present size, but the overcrowding and all the horrors which this entailed continued until its closure in 1853.

In 1884 the land was cleared and landscaped at a cost of £1622 and a strip was given up for road widening. It was opened as a garden in 1885, as a stone on the boundary wall records. Another stone above this one reads:

'This stone commemorates parishioners of St John's Westminster whose bodies rest in this place formerly the burial-ground of the parish and was set up here by the Westminster City Council under authority of the Chancellor of the London Diocese given on the 8th December 1937, the names on the original memorials

having become illegible through lapse of time.
God grant them rest and peace.'

Today, with one exception, the tombstones which remain stand round the boundaries of the garden and most of them are illegible. Appropriately the exception is the solid granite memorial to Christopher Cass, Master Mason, who was mason to the building of St Martin-in-the-Fields, St John the Evangelist (of which he was an original Vestry member) and others of the Queen Anne churches. It reads quite simply:

'R.
CHR CASS Master Mason to his
Maj. Ordnance dyd April 21 1734.'

Another stone which still remains decipherable is on the south side of the garden. This commemorates the Johnson family, of whom the son John became Lord Mayor of London. It is a nice Victorian tribute and reads:

'In Memory of John Johnson and Catherine his wife and their son John Johnson late Alderman of the City of London. The first died June 30 1829 in the 70th year of his age. The second March 27 1846 in the 83rd year of her age. Their son the Alderman December 30th 1848 in the 57th year of his age.
Inscribed by William Johnson their surviving son impressed with a vivid recollection of their ever warm and parental care and in grateful remembrance of his brother's unremitting kindness.
A.D. 1853.'

Here too was buried Christopher Shephard, distiller, who died on 5 April 1732. His tombstone, still decipherable in 1892, gave his age as 146. (It is curious to find in the Register of Burial from 1731 to 1853 record of 109 nonagenarians and seven centenarians, of whom three, one man and two women, were described as living at the workhouse.) There is also record of the burial of an Indian chief who was brought to England in 1734 by Sir James Oglethorpe.

ST JOHN'S WOOD CHURCH, WELLINGTON ROAD NW8

This is an interesting case, where the burial-ground came first, to be followed by the parish church.

During the second half of the eighteenth century Marylebone grew very rapidly. In 1793 one of the churchwardens, George Daniel, commenting on this, said 'the number of burials at a minimum for the last three years amounted to about 1500 per annum', and that the existing burial-ground (in Paddington Street) would not suffice for the needs of the parish for more than three years. Negotiations were opened for a site on the west side of Lisson Grove (then called Nightingale Lane), but these proved abortive. In 1807 the Vestry Board selected the present site, on part of which St John's Wood church now stands, and purchased six acres from Mr Henry Samuel Eyre, which were enclosed by a ten-foot wall. It is not clear how the parish managed between 1796, by which time Mr Daniel anticipated the existing burial-ground would have become overcrowded, and 1811, when the new ground was consecrated, but it is clear that the new ground was urgently needed. In 1823 the number of burials was 1260 and by 1840 the figure had increased to 2328. In the same period the population of St Marylebone had increased from 75,434 (1811 figure) to 138,161 (1841 figure). The amount expended on the burial-ground was £10,743 18s 4d.

In 1811 the Vestry petitioned the Commissioners of Crown Lands, saying that they were proposing to build a chapel within the burial-ground and asking that out of the lands reverting to the Crown on the falling in of the Duke of Portland's lease of Marylebone Park (shortly to become Regent's Park) a road might be constructed fifty feet wide to connect the burial-ground with the New Road (now Marylebone Road) from Allsop Place (then called Pleasant Row). So Park Road came to be built. This petition also asked that a small part of these lands might be given to provide the site of a new parish church for St Marylebone, pointing out that the old church would accommodate only 250 people and that the parish population had grown to over 75,000.

St John's Wood Chapel (as it then was) was consecrated in 1814. Writing in 1833 Thomas Smith, the author of *A Topographical and Historical Account of the Parish of St Marylebone*, estimated that forty thousand people had been buried in the burial-ground. He gives the names of many illustrious people buried there, along with one of whom he thought very poorly indeed, writing 'This notorious impostor was a native of Exeter, and in conjunction with others, had long practiced on the ignorance and incredulity of the lower classes, by a series of the most gross and impious absurdities. It is also lamentable to record that very many persons of respectable condition in life, from whom better things might have been expected, suffered themselves to be deluded by her irrational and abominable pretensions.' He was referring to Joanna Southcott who died on 27 December 1814. This extraordinary woman, who died when she claimed she was about to give birth to a child of divine origin, retained her hold on people's credibility for over a hundred years after her death. She began writing her sealed prophecies in 1792 and followed up this practice, after her arrival in London in 1802, by issuing certificates for the millennium to the faithful whom she 'sealed'. In eight years over 144,000 certificates are said to have been sold, and the sale only ceased in 1809 when Mary Bateman, one of those she had certificated, was hanged in York for murder. The box said to contain her prophecies was not opened until 11 July 1927, when it was found to hold an old horse-pistol, a number of coins, a dice-box, and a novel, *The Suspence of Love*, published in 1796. The followers of her cult, however, claimed that the wrong box had been opened.

To avoid scandal she was buried under the assumed name of Goddard, and even the conducting minister did not know the truth. Subsequently two memorials were erected to her – a gravestone which bore three quotations, two from the *Second Book of Esdras* and the third from the *Book of Habakkuk* which reads:

'For the vision is yet for an appointed time,
But at the end it shall speak, and not lie:
Though it tarry, wait for it;
Because it will surely come, it will not tarry.'

The other monument, a short distance from the grave, was inscribed:

'While through all thy wondrous days,
Heaven and Earth enraptured gazed.
While vain Sages think they know
Secrets, Thou alone canst show.
Time alone will tell what hour
Thou'lt appear in Greater Power.' *Sabineus*

Many of her followers awaited her resurrection and these hopes were revived when her tomb was shattered by an explosion in 1874.

The burial-ground became a garden in 1886 and has been very well laid out. A number of graves with their headstones have been left along the east and west sides; there is a children's playground at the north end and the centre forms a good garden, well stocked and with plenty of grass. There is a fine tomb in the centre of the west group bearing the arms of Major General Sir William Blackburne who died on 16 October 1839 after upwards of forty years in the service of the East India Company (which he joined as a cadet in 1782 and where he was Resident at the Court of Tanjore from 1807 to 1823).

Another tombstone in this group, which would appear to have been restored as it is far more legible than its contemporaries, was put up:

'In Memory of Samuel Godley late a Private in the Second Regiment of Life Guards whose daring and Heroic Courage displayed when charging the French Cuirassiers at the Battle of Waterloo caused his achievements to be recorded in the Annals of War and produced this tribute from his comrades.'

It goes on to record that he died on 16 January 1832 aged fifty-one, and that the stone was established by the non-commissioned officers of his Regiment.

In 1945 the Chapel became St John's Wood Church and in 1952 the parish church of St John's Wood.

Churchyard of St James, Piccadilly – north entrance c.1820.

ST JOHN ZACHARY,
GRESHAM STREET EC2

This is one of three churchyards which lay almost side by side, illustrating vividly how small were most churches in medieval London and how restricted their parishes. The other two are St Anne-in-the-Willows (now St Anne and St Agnes) and St Mary Staining.

It was first laid out as a garden by Auxiliary Fire Service workers during the 1939–45 War.

The church was destroyed in the Great Fire and not rebuilt but it continued in use as a place of burial until at least 1837. It had a close association with the Goldsmiths Company, whose Hall was nearby, and many of whose members were buried here. These included four Lord Mayors, the last of whom was Sir James Pemberton, mayor 1602 (died 1613), whose tomb bore the following verse:

> 'Marble, nor Touch, nor Alabaster can
> Reveale the worth of the long buried man
> For oft we see Men's Goods, when they are gone,
> Doe pious deeds, when they themselves did none.
> Mine, while I lived, my goodness did express
> Tis not Inscriptions make them more or less.
> In Christ I hope to rise amongst the Just
> Man is but grasse; all must to worms and dust.'

Fountain commemorating Viscount Southwood, donor of the garden of
St James, Piccadilly.

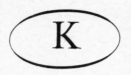

✤ ST KATHERINE COLEMAN, FENCHURCH STREET EC3

This is now a small garden tucked in behind the East India Arms public house. No evidence of either church or churchyard remains except a plaque on the wall of one of the adjoining buildings.

The church, which escaped the Great Fire, was rebuilt in the eighteenth century and pulled down in 1925.

✤ ST KATHERINE CREE, LEADENHALL STREET EC3

Here is one of the best hidden and most charming of the City church-yard gardens. It is enclosed on all sides and can only be reached through the church. It contains what is said to be the tallest and oldest plane tree in the City, and is well stocked with plants and shrubs. In February it can offer snowdrops and a camellia in flower. There are plenty of seats round the sides and an area of grass in the middle. There are other things of interest too. The garden was restored in 1965 as a memorial to members of the Fitch family. Against the north-east wall of the garden the original entrance gate to the churchyard from Leadenhall Street has been re-erected. This is inscribed as follows:

> 'This Gate was builte at the cost and charges of William Avenon Citezen and Gouldsmith of London who died in December Anno Dni 1631.'

and below:

> 'The Fitch Garden was dedicated to all those who work in this

City and to the Memory of James Fitch 1762–1818 who at Midsummer 1784 opened his cheesemonger's shop East of the Church of Saint Katherine Cree, his nephew George Fitch 1780–1842 and his direct descendants Frederick Fitch 1814–1909 Edwin Frederick Fitch c.c. 1839–1916 Stanley Fox Fitch 1867–1930 and Hugh Bernard Fitch c.c. 1873–1962 all Citizens and Freemen of London and successive Principals of the firm now known as Fitch Lovell Ltd.'

In the tympanum of the arch is a shrouded skeleton of stone, and below the gate is a griffin-like animal holding what appears to be a bent sword in its mouth.

There are three family vaults in the grass and two tombstones against one wall.

The inscription on one of the vaults, that of the Middleton family, illustrates the curious eighteenth-century practice of passing on the Christian name of a deceased infant to the next arrival. It also illustrates the far greater uncertainty of human life in that century – four children predeceasing their father, who himself died aged forty-six, and only one child reaching a mature age. It reads:

'John Middleton died 30 March 1732 aged 46.
and of his four children
Mary Middleton died 27 December 1710
Lydia Middleton died 10 July 1722
Lydia Middleton died 13 January 1721/4.
one died unbaptised.'

Added later

'Loyd Middleton died 13 May 1750 aged 36.
Jasper Gale Middleton died 10 October 1774 aged 36.
Elizabeth Middleton died 25 February 1792 aged 75.'

On the side of the vault is another inscription, which is becoming illegible, to the effect that Gale Middleton left £500 £3% stock to Aldgate Ward School on condition that the tomb was kept in repair.

Others to be buried here were Sir Nicholas Throkmorton (died 1571),

Chamberlain of England and Queen Elizabeth's Ambassador to France; Sir John Gayer, Fishmonger, Lord Mayor 1646 (died 1649 in the Tower of London where he had been imprisoned as a Royalist), who is remembered in this church to this day for the bequest of £200 for the preaching of a sermon on 16 October annually to mark his escape from a lion whilst in Turkey, his escape being attributed to his falling on his knees in prayer in the face of the animal. It is also considered likely that Hans Holbein the Younger (died 1543 of an epidemic in the neighbouring house of Sir Thomas Audley) was buried here.

This churchyard is known to have been one of those in which, in medieval times, miracle plays or mysteries were performed. This practice continued until well into the sixteenth century, when the advent of the modern theatre – the first theatre in London being built in 1575–6 – brought their performances to an end.

This church is another example of a parish church being built within monastic grounds to enable the laity to worship separately from the monks. Queen Matilda, the wife of Henry I, founded an Augustinian priory of the Holy Trinity, called Christ Church (a name subsequently corrupted into Cree Church) in 1108. The parish church was built in the priory churchyard some time before 1280, and it is probable that the present churchyard garden was originally part of the priory graveyard. This at least is what Stow thought. The parish church was rebuilt at the end of the fifteenth century, Sir John Percivall, merchant taylor and Lord Mayor 1498, leaving money for the building of the tower, which remains today. This priory was the first to surrender to Henry VIII – in 1531. The King passed it on to Sir Thomas Audley for services rendered. The latter offered the priory church to the parish so that he could take over and demolish the existing parish church, with its valuable frontage to Leadenhall Street, but the parishioners refused the bargain. The church was again rebuilt in 1628–30 (the old tower being retained) and consecrated in 1631 by Laud, then Bishop of London.

✣ ST LAWRENCE POUNTNEY EC4

This church and its churchyard provide two small gardens lying between Laurence Pountney Lane and Laurence Pountney Hill. The church, which stood on the northern of the two sites, was destroyed in the Great Fire and not rebuilt, but its name and that of its principal benefactor – Sir John Poultney – have been well preserved, albeit slightly corrupted, in the neighbouring street names. Both sites continued to be used for burials until the nineteenth century.

Sir John Poultney, draper, who was buried in St Paul's, was Lord Mayor four times – in 1330, 1331, 1333 and 1336. He was a great public benefactor. He founded 'a college of Jesus and Corpus Christi for a master and seven chaplains' to be attached to the eleventh-century church which stood here. In addition he:

> 'built the parish church called Little Allhallowes, in Thames Street; [and] the Carmelite friars church in Coventry; he gave relief to the prisoners in Newgate and in the Fleet, and ten shillings a year to St Giles' Hospital by Oldborne for ever, and other legacies too long to rehearse.'

Stow mentions that the weavers brought from Flanders by Edward III used to hold their meetings in this churchyard, but as he says, 'being in short time worn out', they yielded place in Cannon Street (then known as Candlewright – or Candlewick – Street) to 'rich drapers, sellers of woollen cloth'.

⚘ ST LEONARD, FOSTER LANE EC2

This churchyard is now part of the garden of St Botolph, Aldersgate.

⚘ ST LUKE, SYDNEY STREET, CHELSEA SW3

St Luke and Holy Trinity, Brompton were the only two churches built in Central London in the nineteenth century which had churchyards of their own.

St Luke was built to become the parish church of a rapidly expanding neighbourhood for which All Saints (Chelsea Old Church) had become too small. It was consecrated in 1824, the foundation stone having been laid by the Duke of Wellington, whose brother the Rev Gerald Wellesley moved over from the old church to become the first Rector of the new one.

Like Holy Trinity, Brompton it had a large churchyard of which the northern half has now become a playground and the southern half a good garden.

The churchyard fulfilled its normal purpose for some thirty years. Twenty years later it became the scene of a tragedy sensational at the time of its occurrence. In 1874, when the neighbouring Cremorne Gardens were still flourishing, it was announced that Monsieur de Groof, the Flying Man, would fly out of the Gardens. This he indeed did, suspended from a balloon in a birdlike flying machine with wings which flapped at the control of the pilot. Unfortunately the balloon did not rise quickly enough and it became apparent that the bird was going to alight on the tower of St Luke's, which is some 142 feet high. The balloonist therefore cut the Flying Man adrift in the hope that he would be able to descend into the churchyard. Sadly he was unable to reach it, fell short into Sydney Street and was killed.

ST MAGNUS THE MARTYR,
LOWER THAMES STREET EC3

Today the church of St Magnus the Martyr is overshadowed by the approach to Sir John Rennie's 'new' London Bridge built in the 1830s and by Adelaide House erected in 1924–5. For most of its life, however, the church has been the dominant feature of the neighbourhood, standing on the waterfront confronting for centuries the only bridge across the Thames – 'old London Bridge', the building of which was begun by Peter of Cole Church in 1176 and which stood until 1831. The original church was built in the eleventh century of stone, a rare material then, and was probably one of the finest of the early City churches.

All that remains of a churchyard today is a small paved courtyard at the west entrance to the church. It is not much to look at but in past centuries history has flowed over it.

The approach to old London Bridge ran directly past the western entrance to the church and, as a tablet in the churchyard records, 'this churchyard formed part of the approach to old London Bridge 1176 to 1831'. Over this yard for some seven hundred years must have passed all those who came to the City from the south – friends, rebels and foreigners. In these circumstances it is not surprising that 'St Magnus Corner' became one of those points in the medieval City where things happened and people congregated. After the failure of Sir Thomas Wyatt to get his rebels across the bridge in 1554, three of them were hanged on this spot. When the bridge was almost destroyed by fire in 1633 the church too was almost destroyed. Thirty years later, standing so close 'unto the place where the said fire so unhappily began' as the inscription on the Monument puts it, the church was engulfed in the Great Fire.

87

At the beginning of the reign of George III it was decided to pull down the houses on the bridge and to build a footpath, but a problem arose because a footpath over the bridge was no use unless it could be extended into the City and the western end of the church stood in the way. To overcome this difficulty it was necessary to obtain an Act of Parliament which authorized the acquisition of the most western bay of each aisle of the church, moving the entrance to the church from the west side of the tower to the east side and running the footpath under the tower through what had been the church. The Act also provided that the land taken from the church for the widening was 'to be considered, and may, at all times to come, be used as part of the cemetery of the said church ... but if the pavement thereof be broken up on account of the burying of any persons, the same shall be ... made good, from time to time, by the churchwardens'. In 1825, when plans were being made for the building of the 'new' London Bridge, it became necessary for the church to make a further sacrifice and to give up its burial-ground in Church Yard Alley. In substitution it had restored to it the land taken for the previous widening and was also given part of the approach lands to the east of the old bridge.

The churchyard now contains some stones from the first arch of old London Bridge, uncovered in 1920 when Adelaide House was being built, and a block of granite from Sir John Rennie's bridge which stood from 1831 to 1971. There is also a piece of timber found in Fish Street which is believed to be a piece of the Roman wharf.

Of those buried here Stow records, amongst others, Sir John Blunt, Mayor 1301 to 1307; Henry Yevele, freemason to Edward III, Richard II and Henry IV (died 1400), who was concerned in the building of Canterbury Cathedral, Westminster Abbey and Westminster Hall; and 'John Couper, fishmonger, alderman, who was put by for his turn of mayoralty 1584'. Miles Coverdale, Bishop of Exeter (died 1568), who translated the Bible into English, was reburied here in 1840. He was Rector of the church from 1564 to 1566 but was buried in St Bartholomew-by-the-Exchange and only moved when that church was demolished.

✣ ST MARGARET, LOTHBURY EC2

This little garden on the north side of the church is shared with the Bank of England, which owns the adjoining premises to the north. It can be reached through the church or by St Margaret's Close. It is very secluded – private and quiet. The church, rebuilt by Wren in 1690, has recently been undergoing major repairs and the opportunity was taken to rid the garden of its unduly large plane tree and to refurbish it.

Hugh Clopton, Mercer, Lord Mayor 1941 (died 1496), who 'built the great stone bridge at Stratford upon Haven Warwickshire' was buried here.

✣ ST MARGARET, WESTMINSTER SW1

St Margaret's churchyard was closed for burials in 1853, but it was not until after the appointment of Dean F. W. Farrar as Rector in 1876 that any visible benefit was obtained from the closure.

Dean Farrar, grandfather of Field Marshal Lord Montgomery of Alamein and author of *Eric, or Little by Little*, was by all accounts a man of indefatigable energy. On his appointment he found the church in a neglected state with only a minute congregation and the churchyard, in his words, 'a chaos of broken, unsightly, half-sunken and obliterated tomb-stones, forming the most neglected approach to any Cathedral in the world'. It is recorded that the Abbey choirboys used to spend their time between services in 'sailing their toy boats in puddles made by the sinking of the gravestones, or, if it were dry weather, in playing marbles on the flat slabs of the mouldering altar-tombs'. Confirmation of the state of the churchyard some hundred years earlier is afforded by the poet William Cowper, who was a boy at Westminster School from 1742 to 1749. Writing in 1816 he recalls how, when at school, 'crossing St Margaret's churchyard late one evening, I saw a glimmer of light in the midst of it, which excited my curiosity. Just as I arrived at the spot, a gravedigger, who was at work by the light of his lantern, threw up a skull which struck me on the leg. This little incident was an alarm to my conscience;

for that event may be numbered among the best religious documents I received at Westminster.'

Dean Farrar raised £30,000 for the restoration and refurnishing of the church and transformed the churchyard by raising the surface six feet and burying the tombstones. The result is the beautiful green sward which now frames both the Abbey and the church. One tombstone survives – that of Alexander Davies who died of the plague in 1665 at the age of thirty and of his wife who survived until 1717. He had inherited Ebury Manor (the Grosvenor Estate of today) from his great-uncle Hugh Awdeley, which his only child Mary was to bring as her dowry on her marriage to a young Cheshire baronet, Sir Thomas Grosvenor.

The church of St Margaret was built within the precincts of the Abbey to provide a place of worship for the laity. It stands under the shadow of the Houses of Parliament and became, in 1614, the parish church of the Commons. Its churchyard in consequence does not lack history.

From Saxon times until the reign of King James I the churchyard, as part of the precincts, carried the privilege of sanctuary for any fugitives who could reach it, whence, as Stow puts it, 'it hath not been lawful for any prince or other to take any person that fled thither for any cause'.

In 1303 the Treasury of the Abbey was robbed, the ringleader being Richard de Poldicote, who was subsequently hanged for his part in the crime. Part of the proceeds of the robbery was said to have been hidden in a crop of hemp grown in the churchyard and more was concealed behind tombstones.

In 1555 a monk of Ely committed here the appalling crime of sacrilege, for which he was sentenced to be burned at the stake but first to have his offending hand struck off. This tragic and gruesome story was recorded in the diary of Henry Machyn, a citizen of London, and comes vividly to life in the phonetic spelling which he employed. He wrote:

'The xiiij day of Aprell, the wyche was Ester day, at sant Margatt parryche at Westmynster, after masse was done, one of the menysters a prest of the abbey dyd helpe hym that was the menyster to the pepull who where reseyvyng of the blessed sacrament of the lors Jhesus Cryst, ther cam into the chyrche

90

a man that was a monk of Elly, the wyche was marryed to a wyff: the sam day ther that sam man sayd to the menyster, What doyst thow gyff them? and as sone as he had spokyn he draw his wod-knyffe, and hyt the prest on the hed and struck hym a grett blowe, and after ran after hym and struck hym on the hand, and clayffe ys hand a grett way, and after on the harme a grett wond; and thar was syche a cry and showtt as has not byne; and after he was taken and cared to presun, and after examynd wherfor he dyd ytt. The xx day of Aprell was arraynyd at Powlles afor the bysshope of London and many odur and my lord cheyffe justys and my lord mayre and the shreyffes; ys name was master Flower, alias Branch; he was a monke of Ely; and ther was a goodly sermon, and after he was cast and condemnyd to have ys hand that hurt the prest cut off ere he should suffer, and after dysgracyd, and after cared to Nuwgatt. The xxiiij day of Aprell was the same man cared to Westmynster that dyd hurt the prest, and had ys hand stryken of at the post, and after he was bornyd aganst sant Margett chyrche with-out the cherchy-yard.'

The burning is depicted in Foxe's *Book of Martyrs*, as he was considered a martyr for refusing at his trial to purchase his life by recanting his Protestant beliefs.

After the Restoration of King Charles II the Royalists considered that a number of people who had been buried in the Abbey during the Interregnum were unworthy of such a high honour and accordingly, in 1661, the corpses of these people were taken out of the Abbey and subjected to the indignity of burial in a mass grave in the churchyard. They included John Pym, the great Parliamentarian (died 1643); Thomas May, the Parliamentary historian (died 1650); the famous Admiral Blake (died 1657); and the mother of Oliver Cromwell.

In 1670 there was a dispute between the Dean and Chapter and a Mr Warder who claimed the right to drive carts and carriages through the churchyard. This, the authorities considered, was likely to result in 'routing the graves and discovering and tearing up the corpses of persons interred therein'. In consequence they closed the churchyard to all persons save householders living within the churchyard who were given a key to a door in the south wall. At this time there were, as clearly appears in Norden's Map of Westminster published in 1593, a number of houses lining the inside of the precinct walls; this continued until well into the eighteenth century.

Amongst those buried in St Margaret were William Caxton (died 1491); John Skelton, poet laureate (died 1529); Sir Walter Raleigh, who was beheaded in New Palace Yard in 1618 and buried under the High Altar; Katherine Milton, the second wife of John Milton (died February 1658) and their child (died March 1658); and Thomas Southerne, poet and playwright (died 1746).

ST MARTIN-IN-THE-FIELDS, TRAFALGAR SQUARE WC2

There has been a place of worship on the site of St Martin's for some 750 years, although it did not become a parish church until the reign of Henry VIII. Until then St Margaret, Westminster had been the parish church and St Martin a chapel affiliated to the Abbey. It is said that Queen Anne Boleyn objected to the bodies of those who had died from the plague being carried past the Palace of Whitehall to be buried at St Margaret and so St Martin was 'promoted'.

The position in regard to the churchyard of St Martin is peculiar. Unlike its neighbours, St Margaret and St Giles, St Martin has retained no grass or garden round its walls. Situated where it is, it is not surprising that it has lost most of its churchyard, but it is sad that all that remains is the asphalted area covering its famous crypt. An inscription on the north wall says: 'These catacombs were constructed at the expense of the Commissioners of His Majesty's Woods and Forests in exchange for part of the burial-ground of this parish on the south side of the church, given up for public improvements, and were consecrated by the Lord Bishop of London on the 7th day of June 1831.' The coffins from the burial-ground were transferred to the vaults.

As St Martin became for a time the royal parish church, a number of famous people were buried there or in one of its burial-grounds. Perhaps two of the most interesting were Nell Gwynne (died 1687), and Jack Sheppard the highwayman (died 1742, aged twenty-two). Sheppard was executed at Tyburn on 16 November and so famous were his escapades and his escapes that 200,000 people are said to have been there to watch, perhaps hoping to see another miraculous escape. Others were Sir Nicholas Bacon, the father of Sir Francis Bacon (died 1579); John Hampden (died 1696); Farquhar, the playwright (died 1707); Roubiliac, the sculptor (died 1762); and Thomas Chippendale (died 1779).

St Martin was one of the first churches to seek burial-grounds away from the churchyard. As early as 1668 it acquired a large ground nearby on the south side of Irving Street (then known by its more rural name of Dirty Lane). A subsequent burial-ground was bought further in the country at the end of the eighteenth century, and, just as its neighbour St James, Piccadilly went to the Hampstead Road, St Martin moved to Pratt Street, Camden Town. In addition another ground was obtained in Drury Lane. The burial-ground in Irving Street has long since been built over, but the other two survive, although the chapel on the Pratt Street site was demolished in 1805.

ST MARTIN'S GARDENS, PRATT STREET, CAMDEN TOWN NW1

This eighteenth-century burial-ground, opposite All Saints Church, Camden Town, formerly the parish church but now used by the Greek Orthodox Church, is a pleasant little local garden with a children's playground.

The western part of the old ground, where gravestones still remain at the rear of the almshouses, is not included in the garden and has become derelict. One or two tombstones remain in the garden and others are lined along the wall. Charles Dibdin, the dramatist and song-writer (died 1814), lived in Arlington Street, Camden Town in the last years of his life and was buried here, as was his widow (died 1835). His tombstone, which has not survived, bore the following verse from 'Tom Bowling' the best known of his sea shanties:

'His form was of the manliest beauty

His heart was kind and soft
Faithful below, he did his duty
But now he's gone aloft.'

A subsequent memorial, which does survive, was erected in the centre of the burial-ground in 1880 by 'voluntary contributions of the Kentish Town Musical Society and other admirers of Charles Dibdin'. He wrote over nine hundred songs, including some ninety songs of the sea. He claimed in his autobiography that 'my songs have been the solace of sailors in long voyages, in storms, in battle; and they have been quoted in mutinies to the restoration of order and discipline'. His biographer in the *Dictionary of National Biography* says that he brought more men into the Navy in wartime than the press gangs could.

☙ THE BURIAL-GROUND IN DRURY LANE WC2

Early in its history this ground acquired a bad name. In his book *Gatherings from Graveyards*, published in 1839, George Alfred Walker, a surgeon practising in Drury Lane and who led the campaign to abolish burials in towns, wrote of it as follows:

'. . . many thousands of bodies have been deposited here. The substratum was, some years since, so saturated with dead, that the place was "shut up" for a period. The ground was subsequently raised to its present height – level with the first floor windows surrounding the place, and in this superstratum vast numbers of bodies have, up to this period, been deposited. A short time since a pit was dug (a very common practice here) in one corner of the ground; in it many bodies were deposited at different periods, the top of the pit being covered only with boards. This ground is a most intolerable and highly dangerous nuisance to the entire neighbourhood. Rather more than two years ago, in making three areas to the centre houses on the western side of this burial-ground many bodies were disturbed and mutilated; the inhabitants of the houses are frequently annoyed by the most disgusting and repulsive sights.'

The aspect of this burial-ground is now very different. There is a playground and a small garden. There are seats, flowers and trees, shady in summer to sit under. It is a modest little place, and, perhaps out of deference to Dr Walker and his strictures, the reference to St Martin has been dropped, and it is now known as 'Drury Lane Gardens'.

❦ ST MARTIN, LUDGATE HILL EC4

The former churchyard, which lies on the north side of the church, is now the garden court of the Worshipful Company of Stationers and Newspaper Makers.

❦ ST MARTIN ORGAR, MARTIN LANE EC4

The churchyard of this church, which was pulled down in 1820, is now a private garden.

❦ ST MARTIN OUTWICH, CAMOMILE STREET EC3

This is a minute garden formed from a part of the old burial-ground of St Martin Outwich, a neat little church which stood at the junction of Bishopsgate and Threadneedle Street until it was pulled down in 1874. The burial-ground was in use from 1538 to 1852. Two tombstones remain.

❦ ST MARTIN POMEROY, IRONMONGER LANE EC2

Before the Great Fire of 1666 two small churches stood almost side by side between the lanes of Old Jewry and Ironmonger Lane, which joined

95

the thoroughfares of Poultry and Gresham Street – St Martin Pomeroy in Ironmonger Lane and St Olave in Old Jewry. Both were destroyed in the Fire and only St Olave, which appears to have been slightly larger in size and importance, was rebuilt – the two parishes being united. Today there remains a small garden in St Olave's Court in which stands the tower of St Olave, but it is clear from early maps that most of the garden originally comprised the site of St Martin's church or churchyard.

🦁 ST MARY ABBOTS, KENSINGTON HIGH STREET W8

There is a good and unexpected garden hidden behind this church. It can be reached through the cloister entrance to the church or from the High Street along Kensington Church Walk or from Holland Street on the north side.

That part of the churchyard which surrounds the church on the west side is still enclosed and the gravestones have been left in place. The remainder of the old churchyard further to the west, which was acquired in 1814, is now partly playground and partly garden. A few tombstones have been left but these are no longer legible; a number of eighteenth- and nineteenth-century stones line the walls. A footpath leading to Holland Street divides the two parts of the churchyard.

The church school is on the south side of the garden. High up on its wall are two stone figures of a boy and girl in the blue uniform of the original charity school. The girl holds a prayer book and the boy a pen and a scroll on which those with sufficiently keen eyesight may read 'I was naked and ye clothed me'. These figures, made of Portland stone, cost £10 in 1716. They were designed to stand above the porch of the charity school in the High Street, which was rebuilt in 1715 under the direction of Nicholas Hawksmoor. The old school was pulled down in 1876 to make way for the then new Town Hall, and the figures were transferred to the new school.

19th century Burial-ground of St Marylebone, subsequently St John's Wood Church.

St Marylebone Old Church and the Wesley Monument, c.1888. The
church was demolished in 1949 when the garden was made – the
Monument remains.

The Wesley Monument – Old St Marylebone Churchyard.

The garden of St Mary, Aldermanbury, the bombed ruins of which are now in Missouri USA as a Memorial to Sir Winston Churchill.

ST MARY ABCHURCH, ABCHURCH YARD EC4

Here is a churchyard which has been treated in quite a different manner, and which it would be hard to recognize without its church as its northern background. It is a pleasant little cobbled courtyard with seats set round it. In the seventeenth century it was a grassy spot well shaded by trees. Like St Olave, Hart Street it was surrounded by a wall, erected in 1622, topped with spikes, having an entrance with a death's head carved over it. In 1733 it was thrown open and paved for the first time. The present paving was designed in 1877 by the parish surveyor Edward l'Anson.

Five Lord Mayors were buried here including Sir Patience Ward (died 1696), Lord Mayor 1681 and Whig Member of Parliament for the City in the critical year 1688. He carries the responsibility for adding to the Monument the inscription (removed in 1830) which stated that the Great Fire was the work of the Papists.

ST MARY ALDERMANBURY EC2

This is an interesting and attractive little garden, memorable too, because what remained of this Wren church after the Blitz in 1940 was transported, when the war ended, to Westminster College, Fulton, Missouri, USA (the location of his famous 'Iron Curtain' speech) – to be re-erected as a College Chapel and as a memorial to Sir Winston Churchill. (A plaque which records this has been placed at the base of the remains of the church tower.)

The site was acquired by the City Corporation in 1966 and opened as a garden in 1970. The stonework of the church uncovered by the excavations has been left as part of the garden, which has been formed from the site of the church and from the small churchyard which lay to the south of the church.

The most interesting feature of the churchyard is the memorial to John Heminge and Henry Condell, 'fellow actors and personal friends of Shakespeare', who both lived in this parish and were buried here. The memorial was given to the nation by Charles Clement Walker of Lilleshall Old Hall,

Shropshire in 1896. It is surmounted by a bust of Shakespeare above a reproduction of the Introduction to the First Folio Edition of 1623. One side of the memorial reads as follows:

> 'To the Memory of John Heminge and Henry Condell Fellow Actors and Personal Friends of Shakespeare.
>
> They lived many years in this parish and are buried here. To their disinterested affection the world owes all that it calls Shakespeare. They alone collected his dramatic writings regardless of pecuniary loss and without the hope of any profit gave them to the world. They thus merited the gratitude of mankind.'

A further inscription adds that:

> 'John Heminge lived in this parish upward of 42 years and had 14 children, 13 of whom were baptized in the church, 4 buried and 1 married there: died October 12th 1630 and that his wife was also buried there.' It goes on to say that: 'Henry Condell lived in the parish upwards of 30 years and had 9 children, 8 of whom were baptized in the church and 6 buried there. He was buried there December 29th 1627, as was his wife.'

Stow records a number of burials in the church including Sir William Estfild, Knight of the Bath, mayor 1438, who:

> 'caused the Conduit in Aldermanbury, which he had begun, to be performed at his charges, and water to be conveyed by pipes of lead from Tyborne to Fleet Street, as I have said: also from High Berie to the parish of St Giles without Cripplegate, where the inhabitants of those parts incastellated the same in sufficient cisterns.'

In later days the notorious Judge Jeffreys, who had been a prominent parishioner, was reburied here in 1693 when his body was transferred from the Tower where he had died in 1689. Several of his family were also buried here. No memorial to him remains, but there had been a tablet in the church bearing the text: 'The Lord seeth not as man seeth.'

A part of the garden, adjoining the Shakespeare monument, has appropriately been laid out as an Elizabethan knot garden.

ST MARY ALDERMARY, BOW LANE EC4

The little that remains of this churchyard, at the west end of the church, has recently been made into a small garden by the City Corporation. Another part of the old churchyard, which lies on the south side of the church, is now a public footpath leading from Queen Victoria Street into Bow Lane. In it some tombstones may still be seen. The inscriptions are mostly illegible, but there is one to John Seale, Merchant, died 1771. Other tombstones line the path to the west door.

Buried here was Percival Pott F.R.S. (died 1788), surgeon of St Bartholomew's Hospital, who, as a result of breaking his ankle, came to give his name to medical posterity with the 'Pott's fracture'.

ST MARY-AT-HILL EC3

This church hidden away between Billingsgate and Eastcheap possesses one of the most charming interiors in the City, but unfortunately its churchyard is not at present of the same standard.

As with St Peter, Cornhill, the east end of the church abuts straight on to the street, proclaiming its presence by its projecting clock -- almost like an inn sign – and with its name painted on the wall. Entrance is through a small doorway which leads to the churchyard on the north side of the church. The church was threatened with demolition for a railway extension in 1879 but was saved by the efforts of the City Church and Churchyard Protection Society. Subsequently it was closed for two years and refurnished; during this period three thousand corpses were removed and reburied in Norwood Cemetery.

Stow records several interesting items about this church and churchyard. Its most famous incumbent was:

'Thomas surnamed Becket, born in London, brought up in the priory of Marton, student at Paris, became the sheriff's clerk of London for a time, then parson of St Mary hill, had a prebend at London, another at Lincoln, studied the law at Bononie etc., was made Chancellor of England, and Archbishop of Canterbury etc.'

Stow also mentions an interesting exhumation as reported by Robert Fabian in 1516:

'In the year 1497, in the month of April, as labourers digged for the foundation of a wall, within the church of St. marie hill, near unto Belinsgate, they found a coffin of rotten timber, and therein the corpse of a woman whole of skin, and of bones un-dissevered and the joints of her arms pliable, without breaking of the skin, upon whose sepulchre this was engraven:— "Here lieth the bodies of Richard Hackney, fishmonger, and Alice his wife." The which Richard was sheriff in the 15th of Edward II [1321]. Her body was kept above ground three or four days without nuisance, but then it waxed unsavoury, and so was buried again.'

ST MARY-LE-BOW, CHEAPSIDE EC2

The churchyard, which still retains its name, lies to the west of the church. It forms a pleasant green square, not unlike a small college quadrangle, enclosed on all sides, and thus sheltered from the noise of Cheapside by the intervening buildings. In the centre of the square is a statue of Captain John Smith, erected in 1960 by the Jamestown Foundation of the Common-wealth of Virginia. It is inscribed:

'Captain John Smith – Citizen and Cordwainer, 1580–1631. – first amongst the leaders of the settlement at Jamestown, Virginia from which began the overseas expansion of the English speaking people.'

He was also famous in his own time because his life had been saved by Princess Pocahontas, the daughter of an Indian chief. He became President of Virginia in 1608. His statue stands here not because he was buried in the churchyard (he was buried in St Sepulchre-without-Newgate) but because he was a Cordwainer and Bow Church is in the Ward of the Cord-wainers.

There are two incidents which occurred during the early history of this church, partly within the church itself and partly in the churchyard, and which, as graphically narrated by Stow, illustrate the turbulent life of London in the twelfth and thirteenth centuries:

'In the year 1196, William Fitz Osbert, a seditious tailor, took the steeple of Bow, and fortified it with munitions and victuals, but it was assaulted, and William with his accomplices, were taken, though not without bloodshed, for he was forced by fire and smoke to forsake the church.'

He goes on to tell how Fitz Osbert was dragged by the heels to Smith-field where he was hanged. He concludes with the following obituary:

'Such was the end of this deceiver, a man of an evil life, a secret murderer, a filthy fornicator, a pollutor of concubines, and (amongst other his detestable facts) a false accuser of his elder brother, who had in his youth brought him up in learning, and done many things for his preferment.'

The other incident, in 1284, reads like a medieval thriller. A certain goldsmith Laurence Ducket wounded Ralph Crepin in Westcheape and fled into Bow Church for sanctuary. In the night certain 'evil persons' – friends of Ralph Crepin – got into the church and killed Laurence Ducket and then:

'hanged him up, placing him so by the window as if he had hanged himself, and so it was found by inquisition; for which fact Laurence Ducket, being drawn by the feet, was buried in a ditch without the city; but shortly after, by relation of a boy, who lay with the said Laurence at the time of his death, and had hid him there for fear, the truth of the matter was disclosed; for the which cause, Jordan Goodcheape, Ralph Crepin, Gilbert Clarke, and Geffrey Clarke, were attainted; a certain woman named Alice, that was the chief causer of the said mischief, was burnt, and to the number of sixteen men were drawn and hanged, besides others that being richer, after long imprisonment, were hanged by the purse.'

ST MARY, PADDINGTON GREEN W2

St Mary, Paddington Green was the parish church of one of the little villages which lay well to the west of the City. The first church was built in the thirteenth century and it was not until the enormous increase in the population of London in the nineteenth century that, like its contemporaries at St Pancras, St Marylebone and Chelsea, it had to cede its status of parish church to one of the newly built churches, grander and more spacious.

St Mary's churchyard has been more fortunate than St Pancras or Chelsea Old Church and has not been forced to give up land for the construction of railway or Embankment, although the present century has brought the motorway right to its doors. In consequence it is one of the largest churchyards surviving. There is a good area of grass around the church and to the north lies a small park which was created out of the main burial-ground in 1885.

The present church, consecrated in 1791, is a good example of Georgian architecture and its interior is full of charm. After the rebuilding at the end of the eighteenth century it became a popular village church and a fashionable place of burial. In the area round the church are a number of well-preserved tombs. There is a particularly good one by Rossi for the family of Basil Woodd. This carries a fine coat of arms on its north side and on the south side a profile bust of Basil Woodd (died 1831), for forty-six years Minister of the Bentinck Chapel, St Marylebone, which was one of a number of proprietary chapels built in Marylebone in the eighteenth century. Close by, on the church wall, is a stone commemorating another member of the family which reads:

'In memory of John Alexander Woodd aged 22 died May 13th 1802 in consequence of a wound from a firework on the night of the general Illumination April 30th. Boast not thyself of the morrow for thou knowest not what a day may bring forth.'

The 'general Illumination' was part of the celebrations to mark the official Proclamation of Peace with France following the signing in the previous month of the Treaty of Amiens with Napoleon Bonaparte. It was after this treaty that the French people made him Consul for life and he came to call himself plainly Napoleon. None attending the funeral of this unfortunate young man could have guessed that the celebrations were thirteen years premature. By an odd coincidence the British surgeon who was to attend Napoleon on St Helena is also buried in St Mary's churchyard.

Nearby is the vault of a family with the unusual surname of Bones. In this area too is the grave of the Roman Catholic, Alexander Geddes (died 1802), writer and historian, who was disowned by his own church for his oecumenical views and found burial here.

In the park most of the tombstones, including some quite early ones, have been aligned along the west boundary wall, but a number still remain in place. Near the middle of the garden is a stone cross which marks the grave of William Collins (died 1847), a well-known R.A. of his day but now better known as the father of Wilkie Collins the great Victorian writer of thrillers, still read today. The inscription on the cross is almost illegible.

In the north-east corner, divided from the main garden by a hedge, three graves, each protected by a wire enclosure, stand together. (The hedge has given rise to a suggestion that they are in unconsecrated ground, but this is not correct, as this land was always part of the original burial-ground.) The first is of the great actress Sarah Siddons (died 1831 aged seventy-five); the second is of Thomas Richmond of Half Moon Street, the miniature painter (died 1837); and the third grave is that of the artist Benjamin Haydon (died 1846). Beside the grave of Sarah Siddons is that of her dresser Maria (Patty) Wilkinson.

Amongst others to be buried here were John Bushnell (died 1701), the sculptor to whose credit stand the figures of Charles I, Charles II and Sir Thomas Gresham executed for the second Royal Exchange and now in the Central Criminal Court, and also the charming monument to Mrs Pepys in St Olave's Church; another sculptor, Thomas Banks (died 1805), and the artist, Thomas Devis (died 1810). There is a memorial plaque inside the church which reads:

'In pious memory of Thomas Devis Artist, Eliza Devis, and Anne Devis (who died respectively in 1810, 1825, and 1838). This tablet was set up by their niece Isabella the wife of Martin Tupper the family tombstone in the churchyard having become illegible. 1882.'

Then there is that other great sculptor Joseph Nollekens (died 1823). So famous too was he in his lifetime as a miser that one finds it difficult to resist quoting the concluding paragraph of his biography written in 1828 by Thomas Smith, Keeper of Prints at the British Museum and one of his disappointed legatees. It reads:

> 'Such, and so numerous, are the works of Nollekens, who will long be remembered, not only as having a conspicuous rank among contemporary Artists, in an era abounding in men of genius; but as having, by assiduity rarely surpassed, and parsimony seldom equalled, amassed a princely fortune; from which, however, his avaricious spirit forbade him to derive any comfort or dignity, excepting the poor consolation of being surrounded, in his dotage, by parasites who administered to his unintellectual enjoyments, and flattered even his infirmities, in the hope of sharing the vast property which death would force him to resign.'

He is followed by Barry O'Meara (died 1836), the surgeon to Napoleon already mentioned, and the artist William Beechey R.A. (died 1839).

This too was the churchyard where Emma, Lady Hamilton had expressed a wish to be buried, but unhappily circumstances confined her to a lonely grave in Boulogne. It contains the grave of her mother Mary Cadogan.

At the time of the restoration of the church in 1972, it was decided to clear the vault to prevent further dampness. When it was unsealed and the earth, which packed the entrance, removed it was found to be full of coffins, a vivid reminder of what conditions had been like before the passing of the various Burial Acts began to take effect after 1854.

ST MARY SOMERSET, UPPER THAMES STREET EC4

This is the latest garden to be created (November 1978). It is formed from the site on which the old church originally stood on the west side of Wren's tower and the old churchyard to the east. It is to be maintained jointly by the Worshipful Company of Gardeners and the Metropolitan Public Gardens Association.

The first church was built in the twelfth century and Stow writes 'in the 44th year of the reign of Edward III, the weavers brought out of Flanders, were appointed their meetings in the churchyard of St Laurence Poultney, and the weavers of Brabant in the churchyard of St Mary Somerset'.

The church was destroyed in the Great Fire and rebuilt by Wren in 1695 – the tower being considered one of his finest. In 1870 an Act of Parliament was passed authorizing the demolition of the church, but as the result of a public protest led by an architect, Ewan Christian, the tower was reprieved – another Act of Parliament being needed to achieve this. The church was demolished in 1872 and the proceeds from the sale used to build another church in Hoxton, which was itself destroyed in the 1939–45 War.

Wren's tower was also damaged in the 1940 air attacks, as, perhaps fortunately, were the buildings which had been erected on the site of the church.

Part of the churchyard was lost when Upper Thames Street was widened in 1968 and some of the tombstones were transferred to the old burial-ground of St Anne, Blackfriars in Church Entry.

Gilbert Ironside, Bishop of Hereford and Vice-Chancellor of Oxford University during the dispute with James II, was buried here. When the church was pulled down his body was transferred to Hereford Cathedral.

ST MARY STAINING, STAINING LANE EC2

This is a charming little garden, well stocked with flowers in summer, at the end of Staining Lane with the Pewterers Hall forming its western boundary and the Haberdashers Hall on the east side of the Lane. The church was destroyed in the Great Fire and not rebuilt, but the site was preserved and burials continued here until at least 1847. No gravestones remain but one of the seats in the garden commemorates 'William Scott Ingram, Citizen and Haberdasher 1915–64'.

Here was buried Sir Arthur Savage (died 1632) who was knighted at Cadiz in 1596 and who was 'General of Her Majesty's Forces in the Kingdom of France at the siege of Amiens'.

ST MARYLEBONE OLD CHURCH, MARYLEBONE HIGH STREET W1 AND ITS BURIAL-GROUNDS IN PADDINGTON STREET W1

The original parish church of the twelfth century was built at the south end of Marylebone Lane a little to the north of the road which is now Oxford Street. Owing to its nearness to this highway this church was the subject of frequent robberies, and in consequence, in 1400, Bishop Braybrooke authorized the building of a new one on the site of an existing chapel standing on the bank of the Tyburn stream in the country further to the north. It was dedicated to St Mary and became known as Mary-at-Bourne, subsequently corrupted into Marylebone.

The new church stood in that part of London which developed rapidly in the eighteenth century; the number of houses in St Marylebone increased from 577 to 6200 by the end of the century. The church was a small one and quite unable to cope with the demands made upon it. In July 1807 an angry gentleman wrote to the *Gentleman's Magazine* complaining that one of the most populous parishes had only the smallest parish church to serve it, with no font, no aisle, and no room for depositing corpses on tressels. In his own words: 'At the time I visited this scandal to our church and nation there were no fewer than five corpses placed in the manner described [i.e. laid out in the pews], eight children with their sponsors etc. to be christened, and five women to be churched.'

In 1770 plans had been put forward for building a larger church and land on the north side of Paddington Street bought from Mr Portman for £3000. Expediency appears to have decided that it would be better to use this land as an additional burial-ground and it was consecrated for this purpose in 1772.

At last in 1817 the new parish church was built in the Marylebone Road and the old church became a parish chapel. It was closed for worship in 1926, damaged in the air raids of the 1939–45 War and subsequently demolished. The Rector, the Ven Archdeacon H. J. Matthews, suggested that the site of the church and churchyard should be turned into a garden, and the result has been very successful. It is a courtyard garden open to the street and enclosed on its other sides by a wall. It was opened in 1954.

The central feature today is the memorial erected to the Rev Charles Wesley, the brother of John Wesley and himself a well-known hymn-writer, who died in 1788. During his last illness he is reputed to have sent for the Rector of St Marylebone and said: 'Sir, whatever the world may say of me, I have lived, and I die, a member of the Church of England. I pray you bury me in your churchyard.'

There are a number of tombs remaining, including those of Clement de Crespigny and of his wife, and of Sir Edmund Douce, died 1644, whose inscription reads:

> 'Here lieth the body of Sir Edmund Douce of Broughton in the County of Sovth: Kt. who was cup-bearer to Ann of Denmark, Queen to Kynge James, and to Henryetta Maria of France, 40 years a Constant Servant in his place, never maryed. At the writing hereof he was aged three score and three years in Anno Dm. 1644.'

Tablets on the wall give a little of the history and tell that here in 1606 Francis Bacon married Alice Barnham, and in 1773 Richard Sheridan married Elizabeth Lindley. Here too Lord Byron was baptized in 1788 and Horatia, the daughter of Lord Nelson and Lady Hamilton, in 1803. Amongst the names of those buried here are James Figg the pugilist (died 1734) and Edmund Hoyle, the author of *Hoyle's Games*. The first edition of this famous book was produced in 1742 under the title *Short Treatise on Whist,* to be followed by ten further editions in his lifetime, enlarged to include Quadrille, Piquet, Backgammon and Chess. He died in 1769 aged ninety-seven. Famous artists included James Gibbs, the architect of St Martin-in-the-Fields (died 1754); John Rysbrack, the sculptor (died 1770); Allan Ramsay (died 1784); Joseph Baretti R.A., the friend of Dr Johnson (died 1789); and George Stubbs (died 1806).

Seeing how small is this garden, it is probable that some of those mentioned were buried not in the churchyard but in one of the two burial-grounds which belonged to this church in Paddington Street and which now form the two gardens known as the St Marylebone and St George's Gardens.

The garden on the south side of Paddington Street is the older and also the larger. It was given to the parish by the Earl of Oxford in 1733. It has been said that eighty thousand people were buried here before it was closed for use in 1857. The reason why it bears the name of St George is not known. Both the parishes of St George, Hanover Square and St George, Bloomsbury disclaim any association, and it is clear that it was given to, and used by, the parish of St Marylebone. It is also the more attractive garden with good flowerbeds, a generous expanse of lawn, shady trees, plenty of seats and some covered shelters. The southern part has been converted into a children's playground. In Thomas Smith's *A Topographical and Historical Account of the Parish of St Marylebone*, published in 1833, the author mentions amongst his record of tombs that of George Canning (died 1771), the father of the subsequent Foreign Secretary, which bore the following inscription:

'Thy virtue and my love no words can tell,
Therefore a little while, my George, farewell;
For Faith and Love like ours, Heaven has in store
Its last best gift – to meet and part no more.'

and also that of John Castles (died 1757) which read:

'Late of the Great Grotto, whose great ingenuity in shell work gained him universal applause.'

This burial-ground was opened as a public garden in 1886.

The other garden on the north side of the street, acquired as the site of the proposed church, is simpler. It has a good central lawn surrounded by a path and flowerbeds and again there are plenty of seats. A number of tombstones line the boundary walls, and the path along the south wall is also paved with them. Some remain partially legible, sufficient to emphasize how many people in the early nineteenth century died prematurely. There are two memorials which have not been moved, although the inscriptions are rapidly becoming illegible. One consists of an obelisk on a square base on which one may still read:

'Erected to the memory of Ensign Oswald Lumley Burnand who died in camp at Chota [illegible] in the East Indies October 25th

1810 at which place a Monument was erected by his brother officers as a Testimonial of their Regard.'

ST MICHAEL, CORNHILL EC3

The churchyard of St Michael, Cornhill is well hidden, and of the church only the nineteenth-century porch can now be seen from Cornhill.

Until after the Reformation the church stood open to the south side of Cornhill with chantry chapels and a 'green churchyard' abutting on the roadway. There was also a large churchyard on the south side of the church along which ran a cloister. The north churchyard has disappeared entirely and the south one has lost its cloister; the tombstones have gone and all that is left is a small pleasant garden, again well secluded and with a few good trees. It is not directly accessible from the church but is approached through a Victorian Gothic archway (dated 1868) situated on the south-west side of the church tower, or by St Michael's Alley on the south side.

The original church dates back to the eleventh century. Stow's great-grandfather, grandfather (died 1527) and father (died 1599) were all buried here, as were his godfathers, Edmond Trindle and Robert Smith, and his godmother, Margaret Dickson ('buried in the cloister under a fair tomb now defaced'). It is therefore not surprising that he has a good deal to say about this church. He writes:

'This has been a fair and beautiful church, but of late years, since the surrender of their lands to Edward VI, greatly blemished by the building of low tenements on the north side thereof towards the high street, in place of a green churchyard, whereby the church is darkened, and other ways annoyed.' [This was personally grievous to him as his great-grandfather and grandfather had been buried in this part of the churchyard.]

He continues:

'This parish church hath on the south side thereof a proper cloister, and a fair churchyard, with a pulpit cross, not much unlike to that in Paule's churchyard. Sir John Rudstone, mayor, caused the

109

same pulpit cross in his lifetime to be built, the churchyard to be enlarged, by ground purchased of the next parish, and also proper houses to be raised for lodging of choir men, such as at that time were assistants to divine service, then daily sung by note in that church.'

He records the burial of Robert Drope, draper, Lord Mayor 1474, a great benefactor of the parish – 'he gave to poor maids' marriages of that parish twenty pounds, to poor of that ward ten pounds, shirts and smocks three hundred, and gowns of broad cloth one hundred' (died 1485); and Sir John Rudstone, draper, Lord Mayor 1528, who caused the erection of the pulpit cross in the south churchyard, beneath which he was buried (died 1531); and Robert Fabyan, alderman, 'that wrote and published a Chronicle of England and of France' (died 1513).

Elsewhere Stow records one of his more amusing anecdotes concerning 'a lusty chantry priest' who had his lodging in this churchyard. He starts:

'Now for the punishment of priests in my youth; one note and no more. John Atwod, draper, dwelling in the Parish of St Michael upon Cornehill, directly against the church, having a proper woman to his wife, such an one as seemed the holiest among a thousand, had also a lusty chantry priest, of the said parish church, repairing to his house; with the which priest the said Atwod would sometimes after supper play a game at tables for a pint of ale: it chanced on a time, having haste of work and his game proving long, he left his wife to play it out, and went down to his shop, but returning to fetch a pressing iron, he found such play to his misliking, that he forced the priest to jump out at a window over the penthouse into the street, and so to run to his lodging in the churchyard. Atwod and his wife were soon reconciled, so that he would not suffer her to be called in question; but the priest being apprehended and committed, I saw his punishment to be thus:— He was on three market days conveyed through the high street and markets of the city with a paper on his head, wherein was written his trespass. The first day he rode in a carry, the second on a horse, his face to the horse tail, the third led betwixt twain, and every day rung with basons, and proclamations made of his fact at every turning of the street, and also before John Atwod's stall, and the church door of his service, where he lost his chantry of twenty nobles the year, and was banished the city for ever.'

In 1657, a few years before the Great Fire destroyed this church, a tent was pitched in the churchyard for the sale of coffee, which was first introduced into England in that year.

🦁 ST MICHAEL, QUEENHITHE, HUGGIN HILL EC4

This is one of the churchyards acquired by the City Corporation after the 1939-45 War, and still awaits transformation into a garden. At present there is just an area of grass in which two lime trees have been planted. No tombstones remain. At the end of the nineteenth century it was being used as a private garden for the rectory of St James, Garlickhythe with which living St Michael was united after its church had been pulled down.

The first church on the site was built in the twelfth century. Stow described it as 'a convenient church'. It was destroyed in the Great Fire and rebuilt by Wren in 1677 and demolished in 1876.

🦁 THE MORAVIAN BURIAL-GROUND, KING'S ROAD, CHELSEA SW10

This is another of the hidden grounds. It is entirely enclosed and the large wooden entrance gates are kept shut, but it is open to the public and all who are interested are made welcome. It is approached from the King's Road at the point where it turns south at its junction with Milman's Road.

The burial-ground stands on the grounds of the great house which Sir Thomas More built for himself on the banks of the Thames in 1524. Parts of the south and west walls are of the original Tudor brick, and in the south-west corner may be seen an original fireplace. At the southern end of the ground a panel has been erected which gives a summary of the ownership of the house until it was demolished by Sir Hans Sloane in 1740. It reads:

'In the year of our Lord 1524 Sir Thomas More bought land here and afterwards built the Great House.

1535 Confiscated by King Henry VIII at the time of More's Attainder.

1536 Granted to the 1st Marquis of Winchester.

1575 Assigned to Lord and Lady Dacre of the South.

1595 Bequeathed to Lord Burleigh.

1597 New fronted by Sir Robert Cecil.

1599 Conveyed to the Earl of Lincoln.

1615 Inherited by Sir Arthur Gorges and Dame Elizabeth his wife.

1619 Bought by the Earl of Middlesex.

1625 Forfeited to King Charles I.

1627 Granted to the 1st Duke of Buckingham.

1649 Seized by the Commonwealth.

1660 Restored to the 2nd Duke of Buckingham.

1674 Assigned to the Earl of Bristol.

1682 Bought by the Duke of Beaufort.

1737 Sold to Sir Hans Sloane F.R.S. whose collection afterwards formed the British Museum.

Demolished in the year 1740.'

The burial-ground, which is itself square, is divided by paths into four lesser squares. The north-east square is reserved for children and the others for men, women and married couples. All the stones are laid flat in the ground so that it has an air of a garden rather than a cemetery. It is still in occasional use.

The only child to be buried out of place was an Eskimo boy whose grave is in the south-west corner of the burial-ground. It is thought that he was placed there because he died unbaptized.

Amongst the men buried here may be found the graves of James Hutton (died 1795), bookseller and Secretary of the Moravian Society for many years and a friend of George III; James Gillray (died 1799), the father of the great cartoonist and sexton and gravedigger to the burial-ground for

St Olave, Hart Street – Church and Churchyard c.1670. The gallery to
the Navy Pew was removed in the 19th century.

St Olave, Hart Street. Portal (1658) of the Seething Lane entrance to the churchyard.

St Pancras Old Church and Churchyard from the South East (c.1827),
before the Victorian rebuilding of the church.

Family Vault erected in memory of his wife Elizabeth by Sir John Soane
in the St Giles-in-the-Fields extension added to the churchyard of Old St Pancras in 1803.

forty years; and Benjamin Latrobe (died 1786), the father of Benjamin Henry Latrobe the architect of the Capitol, Washington.

Along the north side of the ground stood the stables erected by Sir Thomas More, which were converted into a manse for the pastor and a small chapel. They are so used again after a break of nearly two hundred years.

The Moravian Brethren – a sect of 'puritanical principles and pacifist tendencies' – was founded in Bohemia in 1457 by followers of Jan Huss. As rebels against the Roman Catholicism of Central Europe they were harassed and dispersed by persecution, but were not obliterated. In 1722 an improvement in their fortunes occurred when a party of Brethren fled into Saxony and came under the protection of a wealthy young landowner, Ludwig, Count von Zinzendorf. In 1750 he decided to move with his group of followers to England and bought a large seventeenth-century mansion by the Thames known as Lindsey House. At the same time he bought from Sir Hans Sloane the adjoining site of Sir Thomas More's old home which had been demolished in 1740. His plan was to establish a settlement where the Moravians could live together in amity as a religious community. Unfortunately he died in 1760 before his plans could be put into operation. The Moravians were forced to economize and in 1776 they moved into humbler quarters but they retained the use of their burial-ground.

When the Moravians were bombed out of their quarters in Fetter Lane in the 1939–45 War their pastor returned to Chelsea, where he now resides in the old manse. The old chapel has become the chapel of his South London parish.

St Paul's Churchyard – south side from New Change.

ST OLAVE, HART STREET EC3

This little garden, which is entered from Seething Lane, is a good example of a churchyard, which having become a garden, has yet retained its individual character. It is entirely enclosed, the entrance being through a fine pedimented seventeenth-century gateway set in a high wall spiked on top, dated 11 April 1658 and inscribed beneath three fearsome skulls:

Christus Vivere
Mors Mihi Lucrum.

Seething Lane is a quiet street, and within the garden is secluded and peaceful. A few tombstones remain. More than a century ago Charles Dickens was to comment favourably on it, writing in *The Uncommercial Travellers*: 'one of my best beloved churchyards which I call the churchyard of Saint Ghastly Grim. It is a small small churchyard with a ferocious strong spiked iron gate like a jail.'

The vestry, which juts out into the churchyard, was built in 1662 and an outside staircase to the south gallery added. The latter was pulled down in 1863. The ironwork and spikes on the churchyard wall were added in 1814, possibly as a protection against body-snatchers. The church was almost destroyed in the 1940 aerial attacks but has since been fully restored. The present church, which dates back to 1450, was particularly fortunate to escape the Great Fire. As Pepys wrote in September 1666 (on the fourth day of the fire):

'I durst not ask anybody how it was with us, till I came and saw it not burned. But going to the fire, I find, by the blowing up of houses and the great help given by the workmen out of the King's yards, sent up by Sir W. Penn, there is a good stop given to it, as well at Marke-Lane end as ours ...'

The churchyard was originally much larger. There was also a smaller churchyard on the other side of Seething Lane which had a similar entrance gate. This churchyard was closed in 1781. Burials are recorded in 'the New Churchyard' at the beginning of the seventeenth century, although this yard was not consecrated until 1680.

Although it is probable that a church has stood on this site since before the Conquest, the dedication being to St Olaf, the Martyr King of Norway, who died in 1030, it is to the seventeenth century that one's thoughts turn, walking along Seething Lane and through the contemporary gateway into the churchyard. For here the Navy Office moved in that century; first to Mark Lane and then to grander buildings in Seething Lane. With it came its principal officers to live nearby; in particular Samuel Pepys, the greatest of all diarists. How many times must he have walked the same way from his official residence to climb the outside stairway leading to the south gallery where the Navy pew had been provided. Here his wife was buried on 13 November 1669 – aged twenty-nine and in the fifteenth year of their marriage – as the beautiful memorial which he erected within the church tells. Here he followed her thirty-four years later on 4 June 1703.

Here remaining steadfast during the plague year of 1665, until ordered to Greenwich, he wrote in his Diary, with his usual vividness:

'*July 26th.* The Sickness is got into our parish this week; and is got endeed everywhere, so that I begin to think of setting things in order, which I pray God enable me to put, both as to soul and body.'
'*July 30th.* It was a sad noise to hear our Bell to toll and ring so often today, either for deaths or burials; I think five or six times.'
'*and then in the New Year –*
'*January 30th.* This is the first time I have been in this church since I left London for the plague; and it frighted me indeed to go through the church, more than I thought it could have done, to see so many graves lie so high upon the churchyard, where

people have been buried of the plague. I was much troubled at it, and do not think to go through it again a good while.'

'*January 31st*. He (Mr Knightly) is mightly solicitous, as I find many about the City that live near churchyards, to have the churchyards covered with lime, and I think it is needful, and ours I hope will be done.'

For 1665 the parish Register of Deaths contains 365 names: and a Bill of Mortality for the week of 12 to 19 September (which is preserved in the Pepys Library) records 1493 burials in ninety-seven parishes within the City walls, of which 1189 were attributed to the plague. St Olave's share of these figures was twenty deaths – eighteen attributable.

Here were buried John Clarenciaulx King of Arms (died 1427); Mother Goose (died 1580), to be followed in 1596 by John Goose, 'one of the poor pensioners'; William Turner (died 1568), Physician to the Protector Somerset, Dean of Wells, and a distinguished botanist; and Sir John Mennes (died 1671), Chief Comptroller of the Navy and friend of Pepys.

ST OLAVE, OLD JEWRY EC2

This is a small shady garden on the north side of St Olave's Court which connects Old Jewry and Ironmonger Lane. It represents all that remains of the churchyards of St Martin Pomeroy and St Olave Upwell (as it was originally called). The church tower, now used as offices, stands at its east end.

The first church on the site, built in the twelfth century, was destroyed in the Great Fire. The church which Wren rebuilt was pulled down in 1888, only the tower being saved.

Here were buried Thomas Morsted, chirurgeon to Henry IV, V and VI, sheriff of London 1436 (died 1450); Giles Dewes, servant to Henry VII and Henry VIII, clerk of their libraries, and schoolmaster for the French tongue to Prince Arthur and the Lady Mary (died 1535); and the printer John Boydell, whose shop at the corner of Ironmonger Lane was famous for the engravings he published. He was Lord Mayor in 1790 and died 1804.

☙ ST PANCRAS, PANCRAS LANE EC4

At present this small remnant of the churchyard, which was added at the west end of the church in 1379, offers little attraction. It remains in private hands and affords few of the amenities of those churchyards which have come into the hands of the City Corporation.

The first mention of the church is in 1207. The parish appears to have been a prosperous one. The neighbourhood was originally the resort of the pepperers, and then, when they moved to Bucklersbury, of the cord-wainers and curriers. Stow, writing in 1598, says that 'of late' the parish had fallen on bad times, sold its famous bell and allowed its monuments to be defaced. This may be the reason why the church was not rebuilt after its destruction in the Great Fire.

Stow mentions four Lord Mayors who were buried here, including John Stockton, mercer, Lord Mayor 1470, who was knighted on the field by Edward IV for his part in putting down the rebellion of Thomas the Bastard Fauconbridge. In addition there was Robert Packenton, mercer, who, in Stow's words: 'Was slain with a gun shot at him in a morning, as he was going to morrow mass from his house in Cheape to St Thomas of Acars, in the year 1536; the murderer was never discovered, but by his own confession made when he came to the gallows at Banbury to be hanged for Felony.'

ST PANCRAS OLD CHURCH, PANCRAS ROAD NW1

This may be regarded as the oldest churchyard outside the City – St Pancras having been recognized as a parish as early as the ninth century. It has even been suggested that relics of Saint Pancratius, who was martyred in Rome in 304 at the early age of fourteen, were buried under the high altar of the first church.

The present church, which is a fourteenth-century building, has been spoilt by a series of restorations during the nineteenth century. On the other hand the churchyard which surrounds it has been turned into an attractive little park and the site itself is well placed on high ground above the road.

On the south side of the church many of the larger tombs have been left undisturbed and walks have been laid out round them. The inscriptions on the tombs are scarcely decipherable but there are some fine coats of arms mainly of the eighteenth century which can still be distinguished.

The land on the north side, which includes the area used as an auxiliary burial-ground by St Giles-in-the-Fields, has been converted into a garden with flowerbeds, seats, a shelter and a drinking fountain. Fortunately a number of the more interesting tombs have been left in place. Within its eastern boundary, with a certain amount of macabre logicality, stands the office of the Coroner for St Pancras.

Today it is not easy to realize that for centuries St Pancras was just a little village church in the country. Indeed in 1593 John Norden, one of the earliest map publishers, wrote 'Pancras Church . . . standeth all alone as utterly forsaken, old and weather-beaten, which for the antiquity thereof, it is thought not to yield to Paule's in London; about this church have been many buildings now decayed.' He goes on to say '. . . yet it is visited by thieves, who assemble there not to pray, but to wait for prey, and many fall into their hands, clothed, that are glad when they escape naked. Walk there not too late.'

In the seventeenth century the church acquired as a consequence of its remoteness a reputation for being accommodating over the question of marriage without banns and the churchyard a reputation as a suitable duelling ground.

In the eighteenth century the churchyard appears to have returned to its more normal use and it was found necessary to enlarge it in 1726 and again in 1792. On the latter occasion further land was needed, because in 1791 a portion of the existing churchyard had been allocated for the burial of Roman Catholics owing to the large number of refugees from the French Revolution living in the neighbourhood. In 1803 the additional land on the north side was taken to provide a further burial-ground for the parish of St Giles-in-the-Fields (which accounts for the burial of Sir John Soane and John Flaxman here).

By this time it was realized that the church as well as its churchyard was no longer able to cope with its share of the rapidly rising population of London and a decision was taken to build a new parish church in the Euston Road. This was consecrated in 1822. The old churchyard, however, continued in use, as no burials were permitted at the new church except in its vaults. The consequences for the old churchyard, even in its enlarged state, were quite intolerable. It is recorded that in the twenty years ending 1847, 26,676 interments took place. The problem was further aggravated by a serious outbreak of cholera in 1849. Burials were ultimately discontinued in 1855.

The difficulties besetting this churchyard however were not yet over. The era of the railways had just begun. In 1863 the Midland Railway inserted in its Midland Railway Bill a clause authorizing the purchase of St Pancras Old Church for £20,000 as a site for a goods yard, but this clause was rejected and the Railway Company had to be content with the right to construct a viaduct across the eastern part of the churchyard as it then existed. This was not the end of the Company's troubles. When the railway works were begun in 1866 a considerable quantity of human remains were disinterred without any proper arrangements having been made for their reburial. This led to an agitation in the House of Commons and work had to be suspended until arrangements could be made. The Railway Company made a further attempt at purchase in 1874 but this too failed and the churchyard became a garden in 1877.

The following graves may still be identified in the northern part of the garden. First there is the family vault of Sir John Soane and his wife.

119

This is an imposing edifice of its kind, and bears the mark of his work. It was erected in memory of his wife, who predeceased him by twenty-two years. She died in 1815 and he in 1837 aged eighty-four years. The tribute to his wife on the vault reads:

'With distinguished Talents she united an amiable and affectionate Heart
Her piety was unaffected, her integrity undeviating,
Her manners displayed alike, Decision and Energy, Kindness and Suavity,
These the peculiar characteristics of her mind
Remained untainted by an extensive intercourse with the World.'

Sir John Soane is simply described on the vault as 'Architect to the Bank of England'.

The other graves are:

Johann Christian Bach (died 1782), the youngest son of the great John Sebastian Bach. He was himself a composer. In 1762 he opened the Hanover Square Rooms which remained the principal concert hall in London for nearly a century.

John Walker (died 1807), described on his stone as 'the Author of the Pronouncing Dictionary of the English Language and other valuable works on Grammar and Elocution of which he was for many years a very distinguished Professor'.

John Mills (died 1811 aged ninety) who, as his memorial tells, was 'the last survivor of the few persons who came out of the Black Hole at Calcutta in Bengal in the year 1756'.

John Flaxman the sculptor (died 1826) and his wife Ann (died 1820).

William Jones (died 1836), who was the schoolmaster of Charles Dickens at Wellington House Academy, Hampstead Road, which was the original of Creakle's School in *David Copperfield*.

William Godwin (died 1836 aged eighty), author of *Political Justice*; and his two wives, Mary Wollstonecraft (died 1797) and Mary Jane (died 1841). His first wife was the author of *A Vindication of the Rights of Women*. Of their marriage, Mr F. T. Cansick in his *Epitaphs of Middlesex*, published in 1869, had this to say:

'Their sentiments were perfectly in unison, and they both had so thorough a contempt for the rite of marriage, that it was only in consequence of her pregnancy, and the apprehension that she might incur that exclusion from the society of many valuable and esteemed friends which custom awards in cases of this kind, that they were induced to comply with that ceremony.'

Mary Wollstonecraft died eleven days after giving birth to a daughter who was to become the wife of Percy Bysshe Shelley.

Also buried here was Jonathan Wild, who was executed at Tyburn on 24 May 1725, buried on the 25th and body-snatched a few nights later. His skeleton is now in the Royal College of Surgeons. At the other end of the social scale were a number of foreign nobility, refugees from the French Revolution. These included Lewis Charles, Count D'Hervilly (died 1795), 'Field Marshall of the armies of His Most Christian Majesty, General Major in those of the Empress of Russia and Colonel in the British Service', who 'commanded at Quiberon a body of French in the service of His Britannic Majesty where he received a mortal wound as he fought with his wonted valour'.

Two other epitaphs which can no longer be read but which have been preserved by Mr Cansick merit mention. The first is that of the Rev Joseph Dungan (died 1797), which read: 'In him were eminently blended with the enlightened sanctity of a good clergyman the amiable and endearing qualities of the pleasing companion and warm friend.' One feels he would have got on well with Jane Austen. The other is that of William Rutherford (died 1832): '30 years Housekeeper in this parish. An honest, sober, steady man, Boast more, ye great ones, if you can.' In contrast to these Mr Cansick has also preserved, from that portion of the churchyard used by St Giles-in-the-Fields, the following:

'The mortal remains of John Brindle; after an evil life of 64 years, died June 18th, 1822 and lies at rest beneath this stone.'

ST PAUL'S CHURCHYARD EC4

St Paul's and Bunhill Fields were the two great burial places of the City. The famous were buried within the cathedral, but without, the surrounding land provided a churchyard not only for St Paul's but for the three churches which clustered round it – St Faith's, St Augustine's and St Gregory's. From the seventeenth century Bunhill Fields accommodated all the great Dissenters.

Throughout its long history St Paul's churchyard has always been much more than a place of burial and has mirrored the turbulent life of the City. It also covered a much larger area than that encompassed within the present railings, which mark the site on which Sir Christopher Wren built the new St Paul's after the Great Fire.

Its story starts in the year 610 when Ethelbert King of Kent provided land on which the first cathedral was built. This gift was confirmed by William the Conqueror, the Royal Charter concluding with the words: 'For I will that the Church in all things be as free as I would my soul to be in the day of Judgement.'

The first cathedral church was destroyed by fire, along with a great part of the City, in 1087. Ambitious rebuilding plans were initiated almost immediately. Richard Beamor became Bishop in 1107, and as Stow writes, 'he did wonderously increase the said church, purchasing of his own cost the large streets and lanes about it, wherein were wont to dwell many lay people, which ground he began to compass about with a strong wall of stone and gates'. He goes on: 'It would seem that this Richard inclosed but two sides of the said church or cemetery of St Paule, to wit, the South and North sides; for King Edward II in the 10th year of his reign granted that the said churchyard should be enclosed with a wall where it wanted, for the murders and robberies that were there committed.' Stow concluded: 'True it is that Edward III in the 17th year of his reign, gave commandment for the finishing of that wall, which was then performed and to this day it continueth; though now on both the sides (to wit, within and without) it be hidden with dwellinghouses.' The area enclosed by the walls extended from Carter Lane on the south to Creed Lane and Paternoster Row on the north and almost to Ludgate (Old Bailey) to the west and Old Exchange to the east.

Within the enclosed area a whole community existed. In the north-west corner stood the Bishop's Palace, then on the north side of the cathedral came the cloisters, enclosing a plot of ground known as 'Pardon's church-yard' which contained its own chapel founded by Gilbert Becket, the father of Thomas à Becket. To the east of the cloisters was a library and a further chapel by the north door of the cathedral. Then came the College of the Minor Canons and a large charnel house for the bones of the dead with a chapel above. In about 1549, according to Stow, the contents of the charnel house were 'conveyed from thence into Finsbery field (by report of him who paid for the carriage) amounting to more than one thousand cart-loads, and there laid on a moorish ground; in short space after raised, by soilage of the city upon them, to bear three windmills'. The chapel and charnel house, he says were converted into warehouses, and sheds before them, for stationers, in place of the tombs.

One of the most striking features of the old churchyard was Paul's Cross, which stood to the north-east of the present apse. Stow says 'the very antiquity of which cross is to me unknown'. It was certainly there at the beginning of the thirteenth century. Its original purpose, as Sir William Dugdale said in 1658 in his *History of St Paul's*, was '... to put good people passing through such cemeteries in minde to pray for the souls of those whose bodies lay interred there'. With this thought in mind, it was always considered a privilege to be buried near the Cross. However, very early in its history, the Cross came to serve also as an outdoor pulpit and as a place of public announcements. Here Papal Bulls were read, Royal Proclamations made, malefactors cursed, and public penances performed. In 1259 King Henry III caused to be 'sworn in' all persons of twelve years and upwards to be true to him as King. In 1299 the Dean of St Paul's 'accursed' all those who had searched in the Church of St Martin-in-the-Fields for a hoard of gold. In 1469 a Papal Bull, pronouncing a curse upon shoemakers who made their shoes with peaks of more than two inches, was read here. In 1534 Elizabeth Barton, the 'Fair Maid of Kent', did penance, before her execution at Tyburn, for her 'revelations' against Henry VIII's divorce. In 1617 Lady Markham did penance in a white sheet for marrying one of her servants in her husband's lifetime.

The Cross was damaged by lightning in 1302. It was rebuilt by Thomas Kemp, Bishop of London, in 1449. The area of the Cross was enclosed by a brick wall in 1595. It would appear that reasonable accommodation was provided for the Sovereign and a limited number of privileged spectators, but that, despite the length of the majority of sermons, the general public had nowhere to sit except on the ground. In 1643 the Cross and pulpit were taken down by order of the Long Parliament. A plaque in the ground indicates its site. In 1910 a modern Cross, surmounted by a statute of St Paul, was erected near the site of the old Cross. This still stands. It bears the following inscription:

> 'On this plot of ground stood of old Paul's Cross whereat amid such scenes of good and evil as make up human affairs the conscience of church and nation through five centuries found utterance. The first record of it is in 1191 and it was rebuilt by Bishop Kemp in 1449 and was finally removed by order of the Long Parliament in 1643. This cross was re-erected in its present form under the Will of H. C. Richards to recall and renew the ancient memories.'

In the eastern part of the old churchyard stood the first St Paul's School, founded and endowed in 1512 by John Colet, Doctor of Divinity and Dean of St Paul's, for, to quote Stow again:

> 'one hundred and fifty-three poor men's children, to be taught free in the same school; for which he appointed a master, a sur-master, or usher, and a chaplain, with large stipends for ever, committing the oversight thereof to the masters, wardens and assistants of the mercers in London, because he was son to Henry Collet, mercer, sometime mayor. He left to these mercers land to the yearly value of one hundred and twenty pounds, and better.'

On the south side of the cathedral was the Chapter House and what Stow called 'the south churchyard of St Paul's'. Here, he said, the south side of the cathedral was defaced 'by means of licenses granted to cutlers, budget-makers, and others, first to build low sheds, but now high houses, which do hide the beautiful side of the Church, save only the top and southgate'.

Moving along to the west end of the cathedral, there were, in Stow's time, two west towers. The southern of these, known as the Lollards Tower (the Lollards having been imprisoned there), was then the Bishop's Prison 'for such as were detected for opinions in religion, contrary to the faith of the Church'. In this connection he writes:

'The last prisoner which I have known committed thereto, was in the year 1573, one Peter Burcher, gentleman, of the Middle Temple, for having desparately wounded, and minding to have murdered, a serviceable gentleman named John Hawkins, esquire, in the high street near unto the Strand, who being taken and examined, was found to hold certain opinions erroneous, and therefore committed thither, and convicted; but in the end, by persuasion, he promised to abjure the heresies; and was, by commandment of the Council, removed from thence to the Tower of London . . .'

There were other more dramatic events which occurred outside the west doors. In the reign of Queen Elizabeth I the Pope, 'by the hand of some of his Proselytes, fixed his Bulls on the Gates of Paules, which discharged her subjects of all fidelity, and laid siege to the received faith, and so under vail of the next successor to replant the Catholique Religion'. (Sir Robert Naunton. *Fragmenta Regalia*.) The perpetrator of this offence was duly hanged at the gates of the Bishop's Palace, and, after the defeat of the Armada, the Queen came to the cathedral, 'where dismounting from her chariot at the West-dore, shee humbled herself upon her knees and with great devotion audibly praised God – who had thus delivered the land from the rage of the enemy'.

Here too, in the reign of her successor James I, four of the conspirators in the Gunpowder Plot were hung, drawn and quartered before the west doors. In 1612 the same king was responsible for the great Lottery drawn at the west doors with £5000 in prizes and the profit going 'for the good of the English colonies in Virginia'.

Watching against the tranquil background of Wren's cathedral the decorous sight-seers emerging from their present day coaches or the peaceful sandwich-eaters at lunchtime, it is difficult to realize what an active worldly place the old churchyard was. For centuries the name of St Paul's Churchyard had been synonymous with the booksellers' trade. As Stow wrote, 'pater noster makers of old time, or bead-makers, and text-writers, are gone out of Pater Noster Row and are called stationers of Paule's Churchyard'. It may have been a burial-ground but it pulsated with life. No one was inhibited by any long shadows cast by the gravestones. The tide of commerce flowed round the old cathedral and did not stop at its doors. Bishop Braybroke, who died in 1404 and who was one of those who sought to keep out the tide, wrote of those who 'expose their wares as it were in a public market, buy and sell without reverence for the holy place. Others too by the instigation of the Devil do not scruple with stones and arrows to bring down birds, pigeons and jackdaws which nestle in the walls and crevices of the building; others play at ball and at other unseemly games, both within and without the church, breaking the beautiful and costly painted windows to the amazement of the bystanders.' The abuses continued during the sixteenth century, and when the steeple was struck by lightning in 1561 this was regarded as a judgement from Heaven. Bishop Pilkington of Durham denounced the use of 'the south aisle for popery and usury and the north for simony, and the horse fair in the midst for all kinds of bargains, meetings, brawlings, murders, conspiracies, and the font for ordinary payments of money'. Nor were these complaints a matter of clerical exaggeration. The nave was like the Exchange and all manner of business was carried on. In his *Londinopolis* published in 1657 James Howell wrote:

> 'But now that famous fabric, which was accounted the greatest glory of London, is become her greatest shame ... nay some have been heard to say, whereas a stable became once a Temple in Palestine, a Temple among us hath been made a stable; nay, they went further, not sticking to say, that as Christ was born in a stable, so Antichrist is like to be born in a stable in England.'

Indeed the final and most disgraceful desecration took place in the time of the Civil War, when Cromwell's men played games, brawled and drank within the cathedral and stabled their horses there. At this time the following bill was posted on the cathedral door:

> 'The house is to be let,
> It is both wide and fair;
> If you would know the price of it;
> Pray ask of Mr Mayor.'

(The mayor being Mr Isaac Pennington, who was responsible for the pulling down of Paul's Cross.)

In these circumstances it is not surprising to find that the structure had been badly neglected for centuries, although unsuccessful attempts to repair the neglect were made in the reigns of Queen Elizabeth and of James I and Charles I. Indeed at the time of the execution of Charles I there was a quantity of material lying in the churchyard awaiting use. This was recorded in the Inventory then made of the King's household goods (having apparently been paid for by him) as:

> 'Stones at Paul's Church
> Black marble steps 508 pieces £150
> Remaining there still.'

It is reported that these stones were subsequently bought by the Earl of Clarendon and used in the building of his own house.

James I and Charles I did succeed in restoring the west end with a new classical porch, the work of Inigo Jones, but the main structure remained neglected until the time of the Great Fire.

Pepys wrote in his Diary on 4 September 1666, 'And Paul's is burned, and all Cheapside', and then on the 7th again:

> 'Up by 5 a'clock and, blessed be God, find all well, and by water to Paul's wharfe. Walked thence and saw all the town burned, and a miserable sight of Pauls church, with all the roofs fallen and the body of the Quire fallen into St Fayths – Paul's school also – Ludgate – Fleet Street – my father's house, and the church [St Bride's], and a good part of the Temple the like.'

and finally on the 26th:

> 'to White-hall ... here by Mr Dugdale I hear the great loss of books in St Pauls churchyard, and at their hall also – which they value at about £150,000; some booksellers being wholly undone; and among others, they say, my poor Kirton.'

At the time of the fire the area of the churchyard had been circumscribed by the buildings around it, and Wren found himself with a curiously shaped piece of land on which to build his new cathedral, without means of enlarging it and indeed restricted by the new building regulations which required him to allow space for the streets surrounding the cathedral to

127

be forty-five feet wide. The boundaries of the new churchyard were enclosed by the handsome wrought-iron railings which remain today.

The destruction of old St Paul's marked the end of an era. It was the eighteenth century before Wren's cathedral was completed (Wren, who died in 1723, was the first person to be buried within it), and by this time the age of reason had taken over and the old turbulent days were no more. The new churchyard settled down to an uneventful old age. Burials continued until 1854. It was first laid out as a garden in 1878–9 and a few tombstones remain including that of T. W. Meller of Denmark Hill, who died in 1850 aged eighty.

Of the churches which shared the burial-ground round old St Paul's, St Faith, which stood adjacent to its east end, was pulled down during the thirteenth century to make way for an extension of the choir and its parishioners were then accommodated in the crypt of St Paul's. (This is the reason why Pepys refers to 'the body of the Quire fallen into St Fayths'.) St Gregory (in the south-west corner), where the body of St Edmund King and Martyr had rested for three years when removed from Bury St Edmunds in 1010 to escape molestation by the invading Danes, also perished in the Great Fire and was not rebuilt. The third church, St Augustine-by-the-Gate, which was at the east end of the cathedral near the old gate into the churchyard, was also destroyed but was rebuilt by Wren in 1683. It was a victim of the 1939–45 air attacks but its tower escaped. The church is not to be rebuilt but its tower makes an agreeable feature in the new landscape.

The whole area round St Paul's was severely damaged by the air raids of 1940 and 1941. As a result of this damage and of some imaginative town planning a magnificent open space has been created round the cathedral, of which the churchyard forms part. There are three garden areas in the old churchyard, in the north-east and along the south side, where there are plenty of seats. The name of St Paul's Churchyard is now given to the street which forms the southern boundary of Wren's churchyard joining Ludgate Hill to Cannon Street. The open space continues on the south side of this street, stretching down to St Nicholas Cole Abbey, thus, in a manner of speaking, reclaiming much of the land comprised in the original churchyard. There are fountains and flowerbeds, statues and seats, and plenty of room in which to look up at Wren's masterpiece.

St Paul, Covent Garden. Churchyard and West Door.

The churchyard of St Paul, Covent Garden has changed little since it was laid out when the church was consecrated in 1638. It was intended to be hidden away behind the church, which was to be the focal point of the great piazza development by the 4th Earl of Bedford in the seventeenth century; but as Bishop Laud refused to allow the altar to be placed at the west end to permit a grand entrance from the piazza it became, as it were, the front garden before the west door.

Hollar's map of the district, published about 1658, shows that the churchyard was already enclosed on all sides by buildings except to the east where it continued round the sides of the church – then described as a Chapel (it was originally attached to St Martin-in-the-Fields and was not promoted to be a parish church until 1645). The main entrance, then as now, was from Bedford Street via Inigo Place with small entrances from Henrietta Street and King Street.

A wide paved walk, in which lie one or two tombstones now bare of inscription, leads to the west door. On either side is a pleasant secluded garden with plenty of seats. It is well stocked and contains some commemorative trees and shrubs, planted in memory of members of the theatrical world, for this is the Actors Church, a connection which might be said to date back to its foundation. Inigo Jones, the architect of the church, was himself also a theatrical designer.

Amongst the famous buried here were the artist, Sir Peter Lely (died 1680); the author, Samuel Butler (died 1680); the playwright, William Wycherley (died 1716); the wood carver, Grinling Gibbons (died 1721); the musician, Thomas Arne (died 1778); the comedian, Charles Macklin (died 1797) who, according to his memorial in the church, lived to be 107 years old but whose coffin plate is said to have shown him as only 97; the artist, Thomas Girtin (died 1802); and the caricaturist, Thomas Rowlandson (died 1827). Within the church are many plaques in memory of theatrical stars of the twentieth century and the ashes of Ellen Terry are deposited in the south wall.

An early but temporary occupant of a place in the churchyard was the statue of Charles I which now stands at the top of Whitehall. This statue,

The Burial-ground of the Pensioners, Royal Hospital, Chelsea.

the work of a Huguenot sculptor, Le Sueur, was cast in 1633 and was first placed in King Street, Covent Garden near to the site on which St Paul's was being built awaiting permanent erection in a garden at Roehampton. At the outbreak of the Civil War it appears to have been in the churchyard and was then hidden in the crypt. Here it was discovered in 1655 by the Roundheads, who sold it to a brazier with orders to break it up. Fortunately, with a good eye to business, he kept it intact and covered himself by selling souvenirs purporting to be made from the statue. The statue did not reach its present site until 1675.

ST PETER, CORNHILL EC3

This is another of the hidden, unsuspected churchyards of the City. The church proclaims its presence with its bold east façade to Gracechurch Street but the churchyard is visible neither from this street nor from Cornhill whence the church is entered. It is on the south side of the church and accessible only from Gracechurch Street through St Peter's Alley.

Today it is a small paved courtyard without grass. There are some good shady plane trees and a number of seats. A few tombstones line the wall of the church. The churchyard would not appear to have changed materially since Charles Dickens described it in *Our Mutual Friend*.

> 'They emerged upon the Leadenhall region, and Charlie directed them to a large paved court by the church, and quiet too. It had a raised bank of earth about breast high in the middle enclosed by iron rails. Here, conveniently and healthfully elevated above the level of the living, were the dead and the tombstones, some of the latter droopingly inclined from the perpendicular, as if ashamed of the lies they told.'

The church claims to be the oldest foundation in London and to date back to King Lucius in AD 179, so it might be argued that this is the oldest churchyard. In the Middle Ages this church was given right of precedence over all the other City churches, particularly in the matter of the procession to St Paul's Cathedral on Whit Monday which started from this church, so the claim may be well founded. Records exist since 1040.

Here in the fifteenth year of the reign of Henry III, who came to the throne in 1216, fled for sanctuary Geffrey Ruffel, suspected of knifing Ralph de Wainefuntaines in St Paul's churchyard. Having got into the church he 'would not come to the Peace of our Lord the King, nor go out of the church, but afterwards escaped; the sheriffs having caused the churchyard to be kept but notwithstanding he escaped under the custody'.

In 1408 the manor of Leaden Hall with the advowson of this living was confirmed by Robert Rikeden and his wife Margaret to Richard Whittington and other citizens of London who, in the year 1411, transferred the same to the Mayor and Commonalty of London.

The old church was destroyed in the Great Fire and rebuilt by Wren in 1680. Its attractive brick tower and steeple may best be admired from the churchyard.

ST PETER, WESTCHEAP, WOOD STREET EC2

The church of St Peter, Westcheap was destroyed in the Great Fire of 1666 but its site has evaded the developers for over three hundred years and is still untouched today. It is now a small garden with a patch of grass, one large plane tree and some seats, enclosed on three sides by buildings but open to Wood Street on the east, from which it is separated by iron railings ornamented with a panel of St Peter with his keys.

The first church was built in the twelfth century and rebuilt in the sixteenth when it was known as 'St Peter's at the Crosse in Cheape'. The 'Crosse' was the memorial erected in 1291 by King Edward I to his wife Eleanor, to mark the place where her body rested on its journey from Harby, Nottinghamshire, where she died, to Westminster Abbey. It became an object of religious significance, the base being adorned with carvings of the Virgin Mary, saints, martyrs, and other religious figures. It stood here until 1643 when it was removed by the Puritans, 'to cleanse that great street of superstition' as Archbishop Laud wrote in his diary. Throughout these centuries it must have significantly affected the life of this little church. When Catholicism ran high the cross was an object of veneration, but when Protestantism held sway the religious figures became objects of attack. The church enjoyed some protection by reason of the long shop which was built in 1401 against the south wall of the churchyard.

Of the shop Stow records that, at that time, it yielded to the chamber of London 'thirty shillings and four pence yearly for the time, but since thirteen shillings and four pence. Also the same shop was letten for three pounds at the most many years since.' The successors of this long shop, rebuilt in 1687 after the Great Fire, remain today, still small and low, the lessees being forbidden by their leases to increase their size.

The City musicians were frequently posted on the leads of the church, Cheapside being the equivalent of the High Street for the City. It was here that Queen Elizabeth I on her passage through the City was presented, in 1559, with a copy of the Bible translated into English.

Stow records the burial of three Lord Mayors one of whom was Nicholas Farringdon, goldsmith. He was Lord Mayor in 1308, 1313, 1320, and 1323. As he did not die until 1361, he must have been one of the youngest Lord Mayors on record. Stow notes against his mayoralty in 1313 the following 'prices set on victuals':

'a fat stalled ox, twenty-four shillings; a fat mutton, twenty pence; a fat goose, two pence half penny; a fat capon, two pence; two chicken, one penny; three pigeon, one penny; twenty-four eggs, one penny.'

At this time it was not uncommon for a man to be Lord Mayor on a number of occasions. Sir John Gisors was Lord Mayor in 1311, 1312, and 1314. In this last year, Stow notes, 'famine and mortality of the people, so that the quick might unneth [scarcely] bury the dead; horse flesh and dog flesh, were good meat'. Hamond Chalkwell, who like Sir John Gisors was a pepperer, was mayor in 1319, 1321, 1324 and 1325; in the first of which years Stow adds 'John Gisors, late mayor of London, and many other citizens, fled the City for things laid to their charge'; and of the last year, 'the citizens of London took the bishop of Exeter, and cut off his head at the Standard in Cheape'.

It was not until 1529 that it was decreed that no man should be mayor of London more than one year.

Q

QUAKER BURIAL-GROUND, ISLINGTON, BANNER STREET EC1

This is one of the most difficult burial-grounds to find. It is hidden away in the middle of a housing estate and is reached by an approach road leading south out of Banner Street. Only a small part of the old burial-ground, which at one time stretched almost to Bunhill Row, now remains and half of this has been made into a playground. The other half is a small garden containing some good trees and an adequate number of seats.

It was acquired in 1661 shortly before the Great Plague and was subsequently enlarged. Some 12,000 Quakers were buried here including their founder George Fox. None of the graves except his was marked by a stone, and his stone bore only the letters G.F. and was itself subsequently destroyed.

In the centre of the garden is a stone inscribed:

'This garden is on the site of the Bunhill Fields Burial Ground which was acquired by the Society of Friends [Quakers] in 1661. The remains of many thousands of Friends lie buried here including George Fox the Founder of the Society of Friends who died 13th January 1691.'

THE QUEEN'S CHAPEL OF THE SAVOY, SAVOY STREET WC2

The churchyard of the Savoy Chapel has several interesting features. It is still private property and belongs to the chapel which is part of the royal estate of the duchy of Lancaster, and is now the chapel of the Royal Victorian Order. It was in 1284 that Queen Eleanor, the wife of Edward I, gave up the land lying between the boundaries of the Cities of London and Westminster, then known as the Manor of Savoy, in favour of the King's younger brother Edmund, called Crouchback, who became the first Earl of Lancaster, and through whom it passed to John of Gaunt, Duke of Lancaster.

Although there was a chapel here in the fourteenth century it does not appear to have survived the destruction of John of Gaunt's palace during the Wat Tyler Revolt in 1381 and the present chapel should be regarded as a sixteenth-century foundation. It was in the early years of that century that Henry VII decided to establish a hospital here on the site of the old palace. The chapel, which is the old chapel of the Hospital, is the only part which now survives and it has been much restored.

By the beginning of the seventeenth century the Hospital, due to the dishonesty and bad management of its Masters, was a decaying institution and, had not the chapel been assigned the role of a temporary parish church, it seems likely that it would have perished with the Hospital, which was finally dissolved in 1702. Fortunately, during the time when the fortunes of the Hospital were declining the chapel was serving the parishioners of St Mary-le-Strand, or some of them. To make way for what was to become Somerset House, Edward Seymour, Duke of Somerset had in about 1548 caused all the obstructing buildings, which included the old church of St Mary-le-Strand, to be pulled down. When this happened the Bishop of London allocated the deprived parishioners between the parish churches of St Clement Danes and St Martin-in-the-Fields and the Savoy Chapel. Here they remained until 1724, when the new church of St Mary-le-Strand, built as part of Queen Anne's plan for fifty new churches, was completed.

The churchyard garden lies on the east side of the chapel. Except that the tombstones are now all round the sides of the garden, it is much as it was when Charles Dickens wrote somewhat sentimentally about it in *All the Year Round*:

> 'As for the trees and grass in the Chapel garden – they thrive wondrously for London vegetation and gather no smoke – they can scarcely be said to be green at early morn. The leaves and herbage seem chameleon-hued. You shall find maize and primrose in their lights, blue and purple in their shadows.'

Today there is a large fig tree on the north wall, a number of other trees round the boundaries, shrubs, rose bushes and plenty of seats, and the flat roof of the ante-chapel makes a pleasant terrace. Maybe one day people will again sit here to listen to the preacher through the chapel windows, as they did when Thomas Fuller, the author of *Worthies of England*, was drawing large crowds between the years 1641 and 1643.

It will be observed that the burial-ground stands well above the level of the floor of the chapel. This is due, as in so many cases, to soil having been added to the surface of the churchyard to provide more room for corpses. As early as the seventeenth century the surface had risen to the height of the window sills, and in 1721 a retaining wall was built round the churchyard to enclose and support it. This wall was renewed in about 1819.

As this was not a parish burial place (except when accommodating the parishioners of St Mary-le-Strand) it became the recipient of some strange guests. There is evidence that in 1552 burial was allowed here of the bodies of executed criminals after they had first been used for dissection by the Company of Barber Surgeons. In 1665 250 victims of the plague were buried here, and, in the eighteenth century, many inmates of the military prison, which formed part of the barracks. These included Irish prisoners from William III's campaign in Ireland, including the Battle of the Boyne, and also prisoners taken in the Rebellions of 1715 and 1745. Condemned deserters were brought into the chapel by a private door to hear the service on the Sunday before their execution.

A number of more illustrious names may also be noted. These include two bishops buried side by side (it is thought that they both died of the plague). They were Gavin Douglas, Bishop of Dunkeld, Scottish poet and statesman (died 1522), and Thomas Halsey, Bishop of Leighlin in Eire (died 1522). An inscription to the latter, translated from the Latin, reads, 'A man of probity, who left this only behind him, that while he lived, he lived well.' Also buried here are Peter Richardson (died 1586), goldsmith to Henry VIII; George Wither (died 1667), poet and hymn-writer; Archibald Cameron of Lochiel, executed at Tyburn 1753, the last to be executed for taking part in the 1745 Rebellion – an unduly harsh sentence, after eight years, on someone who had served as a doctor and tended both sides; and the painters William Hilton (died 1839) and Peter de Wint (died 1849). In the churchyard may still be seen a stone commemorating Thomas Britton, who died 12 November 1839 aged 101, and also the tomb of Edward Willoughby, 'High bailiff of the Manor and Liberty' of Savoy. The last burial was in 1854.

ROYAL HOSPITAL, CHELSEA,
BURIAL-GROUND SW3

Although this is a seventeenth-century burial-ground it is probable that the first burials did not take place until the start of the eighteenth century, as the Royal Hospital was not opened to pensioners until 1692, more than ten years after the idea had been put to and agreed by King Charles II.

The burial-ground is at the north-east corner of the Hospital grounds, fronting Royal Hospital Road and Chelsea Bridge Road. It is kept locked, but access is readily granted by the gatekeeper whose lodge is nearby. It has retained its original character, is still a burial-ground rather than a garden, and consists of well-kept grass and shady trees. There are several unusual features about it. First, it remains in the hands of its original owners. Secondly, the use of the burial-ground was always limited to the pensioners and the staff of the Hospital and their families. Lastly, although burials in general were discontinued after 1854, the interment of ashes continued – the last such interment, in 1950, being that of General Sir Walter Braithwaite G.C.B. Governor 1931–8. He has a memorial tomb in the burial-ground, as has General the Hon Sir Neville Lyttelton P.C. G.C.B. who was Governor 1922–31 and whose ashes are also interred here.

Amongst the tombs that may be noticed is that of the first Governor, Sir Thomas Ogle Kt, who died on 23 November 1702 aged eighty-four. His tombstone also records that, 'Harriet Ogle his granddaughter aged 14 days is here interred'. Here too was buried the most famous organist of the Hospital, Dr Charles Burney Mus.D., who died 12 August 1814 aged eighty-eight, and also his wife Elizabeth who died 20 October 1796 aged sixty-eight. They were the parents of a distinguished family which included Fanny Burney, novelist, diarist and favourite of Dr Johnson.

The two most unusual tombstones however are of pensioners.

The first reads as follows:

'To the memory of Mr John Carley
Sixpennyman of the Hospital
died 13 July 1777
aged 86.
Mrs Mary Codd wife of..... died 1780
Margaret widow of the said Mr John Carley
died May 1785
aged 52.'

This is known as the grave of the 'sixpenny soldier'. These were men who, in the eighteenth century, received sixpence a day to serve on ships of the Royal Navy to keep the peace between the sailors and soldiers who were being carried for military purposes.

The inscription on the other tombstone, that of William Hiseland, who had fought at Edgehill for Charles I, in Ireland for William III and under the Duke of Marlborough for Queen Anne, runs:

'Here lies WILLIAM HISELAND
A veteran if ever Soldier was,
Who merited well a Pension –
If Long Service be a Merit,
Having served upwards of the Days of Man
Antient but not Superannuated.
Engaged in a series of wars
Civil as well as Foreign,
Yet not maimed or worn out by either
His Complexion was fresh and florid
His Health hale and hearty
His Memory exact and ready
In Stature
He exceeded the Military size
In Strength
He surpassed the prime of Youth
and
What rendered his Age

137

Still more Patriarchal,
When above an Hundred Years Old
He took unto him a Wife
Read Fellow Soldiers and Reflect
That there is a Spiritual Warfare
As well as a Warfare Temporal
Born vi of August 1620
Died vii of February 1732   Aged 112.'

There are a number of other graves including those of two women soldiers, Christiana Davis and Hannah Bell, who were held to be entitled to their places having served as men and done their time.

ST SEPULCHRE-WITHOUT-NEWGATE EC1

Holborn Viaduct has a church at either end, St Andrew to the west and St Sepulchre to the east, the latter built just outside one of the oldest City gates, somewhat oddly called Newgate. Stow says it was so called 'as latlier built than the rest'. Be that as it may, the gate was erected, so he says, 'about the reign of Henry I or of King Stephen', and it was the last to be demolished, surviving until 1777.

There is not a great deal of the churchyard left; encroachment has been going on for a long time. Stow writes that the church stood 'in a fair churchyard, though not so large as of old time, for the same is letten out for buildings and a garden plot'. It was further curtailed in 1760 and again in 1871 on the construction of the Viaduct, when a number of corpses were transferred to Ilford Cemetery and reburied there. What remains today is an area running along the south side of the church, which has been made into a Garden of Remembrance to the Royal Fusiliers (City of London Regiment) and which was dedicated in 1949 'to the officers and other ranks who gave their lives in the service of the Regiment since 1685'. The railings are painted red and blue – the regimental colours. There are plenty of seats and some good plane trees. There is also a flagstaff which flies the Regimental Flag. One or two tombs and memorials remain; there is the family vault of Mr Charles Hill (died 1846) of West Smithfield, the inscription on which is still legible, and a memorial to 'Robert Pope, Painter, died 22 December 1768'. A fine seventeenth-century sundial overlooks the garden from the parapet of the south aisle.

The date of the foundation of the church is not known, but in 1137 it was granted to the Prior and canons of St Bartholomew. It was rebuilt in the fifteenth century and again after the Great Fire and was much restored in the nineteenth century. Unlike so many City churches it was not seriously damaged in the 1939–45 War.

The church was originally dedicated to St Edmund, but at the time of the Crusades its name was changed to St Sepulchre, being rededicated to the Church of the Holy Sepulchre at Jerusalem. The churchyard has seen so much of unhappy death that the change of name may not be regarded as inappropriate. Newgate Gaol stood for some seven hundred years as its nearest neighbour across the street. When the condemned man left the gaol on his way to Tyburn the church bell would toll and a nosegay would be presented to him. Beneath the churchyard ran a tunnel connecting the church with the gaol (it was not filled in until 1879) down which the sexton would go to ring his bell outside the condemned cell, pursuant to the terms of a legacy which had been left to provide for this, and to call upon the occupants to repent:

> 'That you may not to eternal flames be sent,
> And when St Sepulchre's bell tomorrow tolls
> The Lord above have mercy on your souls.'

When in 1783 the place of execution was changed from Tyburn to the exterior of the gaol, vast crowds would assemble here to see the executions, which remained public until 1868, and many spectators must have taken up positions of vantage in the churchyard. Here too in the eighteenth century the body-snatchers were very busy, and they are said to have stored their corpses in the adjoining inn for sale to the anatomists from St Bartholomew's Hospital nearby. In 1791 a watchhouse was built in the churchyard to guard the graves.

It was from the steeple of this church that in 1660 William Doddington, at the age of seventy, jumped to his death in the churchyard below – a tragedy which was famous at the time, partly because he had been a man of some wealth and political importance, and partly because of the manner of his death.

Among those buried here are Roger Ascham (died 1568), the author and tutor to Queen Elizabeth and to Lady Jane Grey; and Captain John Smith (died 1631), President of the State of Virginia in 1608, whose statue stands in the churchyard of St Mary-le-Bow.

There are two objects on the outside walls of the churchyard which should be noticed. On the south-east corner is a small drinking fountain erected in 1859 and thought to be the first provided by the Metropolitan Drinking Fountain and Cattle Trough Association, which was founded in that year. Up Gilspur Street, at the north-east corner of the garden, is a good bust of Charles Lamb, transferred here in 1962 from Christchurch Greyfriars, which stood beside the former site of his old school – Christ's Hospital where he was a pupil for seven years.

ST STEPHEN, WALBROOK EC4

St Stephen and its churchyard are tucked in behind the Mansion House. Until recently access to the churchyard could only be obtained through the church, but at the end of May 1980 the gate in St Stephen's Row was opened and the garden is now available to the public from 9 a.m. to 4 p.m.

It is enclosed on three sides by office windows, which enables the casual visitor to imagine how the goldfish feels in his glass bowl.

A number of recumbent tombstones of the eighteenth and nineteenth centuries remain but most are no longer legible – one still partially so records the death of Harvey Nelson of the County of Norfolk aged twenty-three, who could be a kinsman of the great Admiral, and another that of Geo. Griffin Stonestreet, a Director of the Phoenix Fire Office (died 1802). Stow mentions four Lord Mayors who were buried here and also John Dunstable, master of astronomy and music (died 1453) and Dr George Owen, physician to Henry VIII, Edward VI, and Mary, President of the Royal College of Physicians (died 1558). To these may be added Dr Nathaniel Hodges (died 1688), who wrote a treatise on the Great Plague following his experiences in London in 1665, and Sir John Vanbrugh (died 1726), architect and dramatist, whose works include the buildings of Blenheim and Castle Howard, and *The Provoked Wife* and many other plays.

The first church was built towards the end of the eleventh century on the other, that is the west, side of the Walbrook, the stream from which the church takes its name and which the parishioners were required to cover over in the year 1300. The present church was built by Wren in 1672–9.

TEMPLE CHURCH,
INNER TEMPLE LANE EC4

In the eighteenth century there was still a large churchyard on the north side of the church. Today there is not even a garden, only a small dull courtyard at the western end. This contains six stone tombs and a memorial stone to Oliver Goldsmith (died 1774).

Amongst many lawyers to be buried here were Edmund Plowden (died 1585); Sir Edmund Coke (died 1634); and Lord Chancellor Edward, 1st Baron Thurlow (died 1806).

❦ WHITFIELD GARDENS, TOTTENHAM COURT ROAD W1

Tottenham Court Road would appear to be an unlikely place in which to find a quiet garden or an old burial-ground, but when in 1755 the Fitzroy family granted a lease of land here to George Whitefield it was only a country road running through farm lands and market gardens down to the rurally named St Martin's Lane. George Whitefield was the great Dissenter, a contemporary of John and Charles Wesley, who gained the support of the Countess of Huntingdon, David Garrick and Benjamin Franklin. He was so successful in raising funds that he had built and opened his chapel on the land by the following year. The freehold of the land however was not acquired until 1821 when it cost £20,000. The burial-ground adjoined the chapel. By the time it was closed in 1854 30,000 people are said to have been interred here.

The chapel was closed in 1864 and pulled down in 1890. A new chapel, opened in 1899, was destroyed by an enemy rocket in March 1945. It is said to have been the last notable building to be destroyed in London during the war. It has since been rebuilt. The present gardens, the name of which has been corrupted to Whitfield, were acquired by the then London County Council and the Vestry of St Pancras in 1894 at a cost of £5000 after five years of difficult negotiations and threatened litigation. They were opened to the public in 1895.

The Rev Augustus Montague Toplady, the author of 'Rock of Ages Cleft for me', who died in 1778 at the age of thirty-eight, was buried here, as was the sculptor John Bacon (died 1799), who was responsible for the monument to Dr Johnson in St Paul's Cathedral and that to Lord Chatham in Westminster Abbey.

There was a grave here, which can no longer be traced, on which the inscription read:

'Here lieth in Expectation of the last day,
the body of Roger Griffith.
What sort of person he was that day will discover.
He died 19 December 178- aged 61.'

The history of London is vividly illustrated in its church-yards. From St Margaret's, Westminster with its Roman sarcophagus to Holy Trinity, Brompton – the last church built in London with its own graveyard – these little plots of land have provided a resting place for generation upon generation of the city's dead. Only in the nineteenth century did the population explosion render the churchyards wholly inadequate for their purpose – "pestiferous and obscene," Charles Dickens described the burial-ground of St-Mary-le-Strand, whence malignant diseases were passed from the dead to the living. By 1855 burials in the Metropolis had ceased. Many of the churchyards degenerated for a time into dumps for rubbish and sanctuaries for vermin, but little by little they were converted into the playgrounds and gardens which they are today. In some the monuments still proudly stand, in others they have been swept away; some are dark and mysterious, others bright and open; almost all are rich in atmosphere, reservoirs of peace in a city of bustle and clamour. Harvey Hackman has explored them for many years, delved into their histories, studied their tombstones, noted down their inscriptions. Now in this, the only guide book of its kind, with the help of Angelo Hornack's brilliant photography and a foreword by Simon Jenkins, he distils his learning for the benefit of tourist and Londoner. Even the most expert on London history will learn much from this volume, for most of us it will be a revelation of a hitherto hardly known world.

Jacket design: Tim Gill

ISBN 0 00 216313 6